Feb: 1998.

To my Special
Tens Ambrey, &
All my love,   i

G000232118

A. R. THORNE - 1998.

PLACE NAMES
OF PENARTH

PLACE NAMES
OF PENARTH

Alan Thorne

ISBN 1 872808 49 2

Printed and published by D. Brown & Sons Ltd.,
North Road, Bridgend Industrial Estate, Bridgend, Mid Glamorgan.

DEDICATION

To my mother and father, belated thanks.

Mr Thorne deserves the congratulations of all who
know and have an affection for Penarth and Cogan
for his remarkably detailed piece of research.
His resulting work will add to our knowledge of
the history and background of the town and its
environs, and we shall learn much that was not
already known to most of us.

I hope the book will prove to be a great success.

James Callaghan

Rt Hon Lord Callaghan of Cardiff KG
14th November 1996

ACKNOWLEDGEMENTS

My thanks go to all the people who assisted me with the production of this book, I am particularly indebted to councillour John Birch for his initial and continual support and to the Penarth Town Council for the financial support. And I would take this opportunity to record the assistance and encouragement I received from Edward Vick, Town Clerk, and his staff at West House also Bryn Jones and his colleagues at the Local Studies Department at Cardiff Central Library, and Chief Librarian Marcus Payne and the staff at Penarth Library.

Special thanks go to Andrey Poole and Graham Robertson, of the Penarth Society, who read the original rough draft, Marilyn and Imogen Myerscough, of the Penarth Tranlation Agency who 'battled' to decipher my longhand scrawl and who provided the typed final draft and disk, and Diane Mead and Julian Myerscough for allowing me to use their excellent sketches.

I have been aided and befriended by Bob Whitaker and his staff at David Brown and Sons, and have been honoured by the Foreword provided by Lord Callaghan.

In conclusion I must record my gratitude to my good friend G. Farquhar, and last but not least my wife who has shewn forebearance and continual support beyond the call of duty!!

Thank you,

Alan Thorne

PLACE NAMES OF PENARTH -
HISTORICAL AND COLLOQUIAL

The casual observer could be forgiven for thinking that Penarth's history began with the opening of the Dock in 1865. This is understandable given that there is very little recorded history prior to 1859 when the excavation of the Dock started. Gwynedd O Pierce makes the point that "documentary evidence is less than satisfactory concerning the parish (Penarth) than any other in the Hundred of Dinas Powis" [i] (There are twenty parishes in the Hundred[1]).

Before the mid 1850s, which was roughly when urbanization started, the Parish of Penarth was a barren, windswept area with a prominent headland and ridge that ran from east to west at the northern extremity of the parish, and an extensive marshy, pond-filled plateau running southwards from the ridge towards the Parish of Lavernock. The parish was sparsely populated, with just 72 inhabitants in 1801. The geographical position and the topography of the parish were to play major roles in the development of the town.

Penarth Head, the highest point on the South Wales coast, and Penarth Ridge provided a sheltered and safe mooring place, and anchorage on the extensive mud flats. It also afforded protection against the prevailing westerly winds and from the problems of the massive, twice-daily tidal changes. The Penarth Ridge also provided an abundant supply of fresh water from the numerous, vigorous streams that drained from it. Evidence of this can still be found in the form of today's culverted Dingles, although other streams were lost following urbanisation. The Head and the Ridge protected the vast expanse of mud known as Penarth Harbour. B H Malkin, the famous antiquarian, who toured Wales during 1803, visited Penarth and noted: "Penarth Harbour is the best and safest in the Bristol Channel except Milford Haven, especially for Bristol shipping[2]."

From the time Man first took to the water, Penarth, given its position and topography, would have been visited, and occasionally settled in, even if only temporarily. Early voyagers sought to take advantage of the longest and deepest indentation into mainland Britain - the Bristol Channel and the River Severn - that extends into the very heart of England and Wales. From the time of these earliest water-borne travellers, Penarth would have been at least a port

---

[1] "The Place-Names of the Dinas Powys Hundred", G. O. Pierce.
[2] B. H. Malkin: "The Scenery, Antiquities and Biography of South Wales", published in 2 volumes, 1804.

1

of call, an anchorage, a haven in which to ride out a storm or to wait for a change of tide, as well as an opportunity to take on fresh water and perhaps forage for food in the wooded dingles.

The earliest visitors would have been travellers, first from the Stone Age and then the Bronze Age. Evidence of both peoples are found at various places along the South Glamorgan Coast, including nearby Sully Island, Barry Island and Ely. During the Bronze Age the Severn-Cotswold megalithic tomb-builders, the "Beaker Folk", would have called at Penarth carrying Presceli stone from Milford Haven to Stonehenge. There were Iron Age visitors circa 500 BC, and they would have been followed by the Veneti from the Vannes region of Brittany, who by 100 BC had built up a regular trade route with South Wales.

By 55 AD the Romans had built their first castrum on the banks of the River Taff at Cardiff, and there soon followed villas at Ely and Llandough. The Romans quarried stone out of the north side of the Penarth Ridge, and would have undoubtedly established temporary accommodation on the Penarth bank of the River Ely to house men engaged in the quarrying and dressing of the stone. Small sections of Penarth stone, incidentally, remains of the Roman castrum, can still be seen outlined in the front wall of Cardiff Castle.

Other early visitors included a number of Celtic Saints, Irish and Viking raiders, the Normans and even Moorish pirates.

The place-names in this monograph are a reminder of some of these visitors and settlers, and bear vivid witness to the town's maritime history. They also reflect the town's connections with the powerful Windsor/Clive/Plymouth dynasty, which owned the parish of Penarth. There are connections, too, with their kinsmen, the Butes, who owned the parishes of Cogan and Llandough.

Although the list is not definitive, it is an attempt to record and, I hope, explain the various place-names in use around the town before they are forgotten and lost to us. Many enjoy regular currency, some are only rarely used, while many are no longer heard. This third category is marked as (LOST).

I very much hope the list will be of interest, will entertain, and perhaps bring back for those reading it memories of people, places and events forgotten or nearly forgotten, but which are worth remembering. It may well prompt some readers into recalling place-names omitted from this list, and if this is so I should be delighted and grateful to hear from them.

Copyright Alan Thorne
January 1996

ABATTOIR

The site of the former abattoir can still be seen in Salop Place opposite Bromfield Place, and is today used to garage motor-cars. Mr Harry Martin records in "We Remember It Well", a series of recollections published in 1995 by the Penarth Past Oral History Group, that "a railway truck would arrive at Penarth Town Station (see Cattle Pens), loaded with a consignment of pigs - the pigs would be off-loaded, driven up through Stanwell Road, Windsor Road, then through Glebe Street, Salop Street and lastly Salop Place - where the firm's slaughter house was situated."

ADAM'S WOOD (LOST)

Modern Cogan is almost encircled by an escarpment, the eastern section of which stretches from the Cogan Garden Village around to the Cowslip Estate. The escarpment is mainly wooded and is all that is left of Coed Yr Hebog, the Wood of the Hawk, which used also to cover the area where parts of Shakespeare Avenue, Tennyson Road and Wordsworth Avenue now stand.

In the nineteenth century the wood was known as Adam's Wood. The Penarth Observer of 23rd May 1892 reported: "On Sunday evening a fire was discovered in Adam's Wood, Cogan, the fire burned freely and fiercely. PC Thomas H Evans, the Cogan policeman, and some local men got to work and eventually after much trouble managed to subdue the fire. It is believed the fire was started by mischievous local boys[3]."

The derivation is not known, although the name Adam does appear locally elsewhere, for instance as Adamsdown (Adam's pasture), an area of Cardiff. Adam Kyngot was a portarius (gate keeper) at Cardiff Castle in the fourteenth century and held Adamsdown. It may be that some land was gifted or leased in Penarth, hence Adam's Wood. In more modern times the wood was also known as 'Milkies'.

AFON LLAI LLAID (LOST)

This early Welsh name for Penarth's raison d'être, the River Ely, was in use up until the early nineteenth century. Afon is Welsh for river, Llai translates as brown or grey, while Llaid means mud, mire, or slime. Hence the translation

---

[3] Penarth Observer, 1892

3

"a mud river". From the eighteenth century onwards the name Ely, a diminution or corruption of Llai, became the more widely used name.

Captain Smythe, who worked as a Marine Superintendent to Lord Bute, in part of evidence he gave to Parliament in 1840 stated: "Ely is a diminutive or corruption of Afon Llai, the mud river[4]".

AGNES STREET (COGAN)

Almost all of the street names of the original Docktown area remind us of the two families who respectively held the parishes of Penarth and Cogan, the Windsor/Clives and the Butes. Robert Clive (born 24 May 1824) married Lady Mary Selina Bridgeman on 20 October 1852. They had four children, one son and three daughters, the youngest of whom was called Agnes.

ALABASTER MINE

Most of the published histories and guide books of Penarth refer to the existence of an alabaster mine or mines, although none give any details such as the dates they were in operation, their location, who owned them, etc. A few years ago at a Town Council meeting it was suggested that subsidence in the St Augustine's Road area could be due to the existence of old alabaster mines under the Penarth Head and Ridge. No evidence can be found to substantiate their existence. The site most often suggested, however, is in the area of foreshore below the Seven Sisters.

The alabaster, or gypsum, was taken from the foreshore and from the cliff face. E T Bevan[5] recalls that the 'White Rock' was very popular for its medicinal properties, especially with the folk of the Vale of Glamorgan. It used to be ground down and mixed with water, and Bevan claims that the 'White Rock' medicine was used as an 'antidote' and given to people "who had been bitten by a mad dog". He makes no mention of a mine or a commercial venture at Penarth, however.

Records show that for centuries small vessels came up onto the beach to load alabaster. In the mid eighteenth century, a vessel loaded sixteen tons of the rock and transported it to Oxwich Bay where it was used in the building of Penrice

[4] W. H. Smyth: "Nautical observations on the port and maritime vicinity of Cardiff", 1840.
[5] An unpublished monograph entitled "Reminiscences of Old Penarth", now held in Penarth Library.

Castle, at a cost of £19-4-0[6]. Ironically, in June 1915 the trow 'Eliza' of Bridgwater transported 130 tons of gypsum from Bristol to Penarth Dock at a cost of 21 shillings per ton[7]. B R Keitch, a local historian locates an alabaster mine at the end of the 'Cliff Walk' and notes that there is a church at Baglan built of Penarth alabaster[8].

ALBERT CLUB (LOST)

During the nineteenth century the Docktown had a proliferation of drinking clubs, both legal and illegal. One of the legal clubs was the Albert, which stood at 81 Maughan Street, just at the junction of Maughan Street (now Queen's Road) and the graphically named Steep Street. The club traded under the grandiose title of the Penarth Albert Club Company Limited. During the 1880s and 90s a Mr W A Hodge was its secretary, and Mr Albert Barnett its manager.

The club enjoyed a certain notoriety, mainly due to Barnett who bred fighting dogs and organised dog-fights for prize money, with side bets involving other dog owners from Grangetown, Cardiff Docks and the Valleys. He was arrested on a number of occasions, usually for assaulting police-officers sent to stop the dog fighting.

The club was also well-known for its 'elastic' trading hours. The local press reported that: "Five policemen raided the Albert Club on Sunday March 13, 1896, and arrested about 20 men, the men and the club's stock were all taken to the Police Station"[9].

ALBERT HALL (LOST)

In 1892 Solomon Andrews built a large hall in Albert Road, on the site of a previous smaller hall that had been destroyed by fire. The hall, which was located between Ludlow Lane and Plassey Street, was known by various names including, for a short time, Albert Hall. In the 1920s, the Albert Hall Cinema was opened under the proprietorship of the Willmore Brothers.

[6] D. Moore: "Wales in the Eighteenth Century".
[7] Basil Greenhill: "The Merchant Schooners".
[8] B. R. Keitch: "A Brief Look at Penarth". Unpublished monograph, 1972.
[9] Penarth Observer, 1896.

ALBERT ROAD

This road runs from the Windsor Road roundabout up as far as Stanwell Crescent and was named on 30 September 1889, almost undoubtedly in honour of Prince Albert, the Consort of Queen Victoria. The road had originally been known as the Parish Road until 1880, when it became Stanwell Road, the name it held until 1889.

ALBERT SQUARE (LOST)

This was the title given to the area now covered by the Belle Vue Park and Bowling Green. It was originally glebeland, i.e. land given to a clergyman as part of his benefice, before being acquired by the Windsor Family, who leased it as rough grazing for animals.

A quarry was established in the 1860s, the stone from which was used in house building and for both the National School (Plassey Street) and the Board School (Albert Road). The quarry ceased operations in the 1870s and quickly filled up with water. The water attracted the local children, and there were many fatalities and near fatalities. The school records show that on: "16 March 1877, two little boys drowned in the quarry opposite the school)[10] The quarry was subsequently filled in and became a public space known as Albert Square.

The Square was used by travelling fairs and the occasional circus, as well as for the communal grazing of cattle, horses and donkeys. During the 1880s and 90s the local press received a stream of complaints, especially about the nocturnal braying of donkeys (see Penarth Square). Moves were made to tidy up Albert Square and the Minutes of the Local Board meeting held on 5 December 1892 record that: "Mr Cornwall said he had been to see, on several occasions, Mr Forrest (agent to the Windsor Estate) and Mr Snell (Windsor Estate surveyor and architect) to ask if Lord Windsor would landscape Albert Square and the Dingle[11]."

ALBERTA PLACE

Alberta was the name of the wife of the Earl of Plymouth. Robert George Windsor Clive (born 27 August 1857) married Alberta Paget in 1883. Alberta

---

[10] Log Book, Penarth Board School. Glamorgan Records Office.
[11] Local Board Minutes 1892, Penarth Library.

BELLE VUE BOWLING GREEN

© Diane Mead

The Bowling Green was laid in 1914.

Place links Alberta Road to Sully Terrace. A small railway station was established between Archer Terrace and Sully Terrace and opened as Alberta Place Platform on 19 September 1904. It was re-named Alberta Place Halt on 18 October 1923, but was eventually closed to passengers 40 years later on 6 May 1963[12]. The platforms, public shelter and footbridge have all been demolished, and the track is now a public footpath and nature walk.

ALCESTER HOUSE (lost)

During the nineteenth century the town had numerous private preparatory schools, particularly during the 1880s and 1900s. It was during this period that a Miss Hill ran a small school for Young Ladies from Alcester House, 27 Windsor Road. Miss Mary Ellen Hill's school was in business from approximately 1884 to 1894.

ALL SAINTS

Between approximately 1880 and 1891 the original All Saints, a large iron church, stood on the corner of Rectory Road and Stanwell Road, opposite what is today's Library. A new All Saints Church was due to have been built near Park Road on land donated by Lord Windsor, but the charming site in Victoria Square was chosen instead and during 1890 and 1891 John Coates Carter and his partner, John Pollard Seddon, designed a new church which was consecrated in October 1891. The church was badly damaged by fire in 1927 and bombed so badly it was no more than a shell in 1941.

ANDERSON'S

In 1863 Charles Cooper, a boat builder and a cadet of the Cooper family of Pill on the Bristol Avon, themselves the renowned builders of the much admired and world famous Bristol Channel Pilot Cutters, opened a boat-yard on the shingle strand beneath the Penarth Head just south of the Marine Hotel. In 1900 the yard was taken over by Harold Clayton, who was later to become Sir Harold Clayton, the naval architect. Clayton was Commodore of the Penarth Yacht Club from 1920 to 1926, a post his uncle, Colonel Sir Fitzroy Clayton, had held between 1901 and 1906[13].

---

[12] E. Mountford & N. Sprinks: The Taff Vale Lines to Penarth, 1993.
[13] C. M. Tarver: "Penarth Yacht Club, 1880-1980" (1980).

© Julian Myerscough

Clanton's new shed on completion 20 Jan, 1900. The smaller shed alongside was the R.N.L.I. boat shed created in 1884 at a cost of £250-9s-7d. Clayton bought it in 1905 for £10.00p. Both sheds were acquired by Anderson c.1914.

The yard was taken over in 1910 by Andrew Anderson, who had arrived in Penarth around 1882 as a ship's carpenter on board a square-rigged vessel, the Lagos. Anderson had been born Andreas Andresen in Denmark, but anglicised his name when he settled in Penarth. In 1888 he married another Danish immigrant, Margaret Dippy. Anderson worked on the Dock and then for Clayton until 1904, when he set up his own business alongside Clayton's yard[14].

Clayton's father died in 1913, whereupon Clayton became the 10th Baronet of Marden Park. He subsequently sold his Penarth Yacht Building Company to Anderson. By this time Anderson had four large boat building sheds in his yard -Cooper's original shed, another very large shed built by Clayton in 1900, the original life-boat shed, and the fourth a shed he himself built in 1904.

Cooper had built pilot-cutters during the 1860s and 70s. Clayton continued the tradition, building a pilot-cutter, the Faith, in 1904. And ten years later Anderson, too, built a pilot-cutter, the Nocomis in 1914. This was at a time when the Bristol Channel Pilots were forsaking sail in favour of steam vessels[15].

Under these three owners the Dock Beach complex produced pilot-cutters and private yachts over a long period of time, as well as supplying small work boats to local owners. Between the two World Wars Anderson, aided by his son John, built many yachts that were to become famous in sailing circles. He built yachts for the Neale family, the owners of Neale & West Trawlers, and one of these, the Linney, a truly beautiful boat that had been launched in 1932, was only recently lost when it went down in the Caribbean. Anderson also built two yachts, the Emmanuel and the Caplin, for Commander Graham of Bridgwater, an intrepid sailor who undertook many long-distance single handed voyages[16].

The yard continued in production until the 1950s. Anderson died at Christmas 1950, and the last remains of the yard, the stone foundations of the shed Clayton erected in 1900, together with a section of the lifeboat slipway, were only recently bulldozed to make way for the Cardiff Bay re-development project.

---

[14] Robert Holden, Classic Boats, Issue no. 59.
[15] P. Stuckey: Sailing Pilots of the Bristol Channel, 1977.
[16] Commander Robert Graham: "Rough Passage" (now out of print).

ANDREWS' HALLS, LARGE AND SMALL

The ubiquitous Solomon Andrews, an archetypal Smilesian Victorian entrepreneur, played a principal role in Penarth's early urban history and development. He built his Large Hall (see Albert Hall) in 1892 on the site of an earlier and smaller hall which had been destroyed by fire. The hall was used at various times for public meetings, political meetings, religious services, dances, concerts, and it later became a music hall cinema. In the 1920s it was used by Rupert Batten to present operettas and musical comedies.

Dame Clara Novello Davies, mother of Ivor Novello, gave numerous concerts in Penarth to raise money for the building of the Bethania Chapel in Hickman Road (recently demolished). On 31 March 1893 she gave a recital at Andrew's Large Hall.

In 1893 the local press reported that Taff Vale Railway employees were dissatisfied with their wages and that "200 TVR servants headed by the Cogan Military Band marched to Andrew's Hall to hold a meeting presided over by Mr John Cooke, to discuss their grievances against the TVR management". (A well known Penarthian, Mr Lester Cross, now deceased, was often heard to say "The wages of sin are death; the wages of the TVR are slow starvation".)

Andrews' Small Hall, sometimes referred to as the Lesser Hall, was built during the 1870s and can still be seen. It is now used as the Snooker Hall in Ludlow Lane. This hall was also used for dances, parties, meetings and by various religious sects who had no premises of their own, including the Salvation Army, the Welsh Calvinists and others.

During the latter part of 1910 both halls were granted cinematic licences, both issued to a Mr Jones, who leased them from the Andrews Estate.

ANDREW ROAD

Andrew Road was cut into the western escarpment that forms part of the Cogan glacial bowl in the 1890s. The work was carried out under the aegis of the Marquis of Bute, the owner of the parishes of Cogan and Llandough, the intention being to shorten the route from Cogan to Llandough. The road may have been named after Andrew Corbett, the son of J S Corbett of Cogan Pill House (now the Beefeater restaurant) who was a kinsman of Lord Bute and the Earl's local agent. It might also have commemorated Andrew, the Seventh Earl of Plymouth, who was born in 1789 and who died, unmarried, on 19 January 1837.

ANGEL MEWS (LOST)

The original Docktown abounded with stables designed for commercial use as opposed to the large private stables serving the town's villas and mansions which were built during the later stages of urbanisation in the 1880s and 1890s. Many of the Docktown stables are still standing today. Some can be found alongside rows of terraced houses in the old Docktown, others are tucked away in the labyrinth of lanes that run north of Windsor Road.

Angel Mews, which were located between numbers 52 and 53 Salop Street, were the premises of Mr E A Hooper, who advertised himself as a Cab Proprietor and Funeral Furnisher. Coffins were made and stored in the roomy lofts, while the horses, cabs and hearses were kept below. The extensive buildings and yard have recently been tastefully restored.

ARCHER TERRACE

Other Lewis, the Fourth Earl of Plymouth, was born in 1731. In 1750 he married Katherine, daughter of Thomas, Lord Archer. They had three sons, Other, Andrew and Henry. The eldest son, Other Hickman, who inherited his father's title and became the Fifth Earl of Plymouth, married Sarah, sister of Andrew, Lord Archer. After Hickman's death, his widow married William Pitt, Earl Amherst. When the houses in Archer Terrace were first built they were known as Westbourne Terrace.

ARCOT CLUB (LOST)

The Arcot was one of the many drinking clubs to be found in the nineteenth century Docktown. During the 1870s and 80s it occupied number 22 Arcot Street, on the corner with Salop Street. The club manager was Chas Newman.

ARCOT SHRUBBERY

This small triangle of land at the northern end of Arcot Street was one of the many open spaces gifted to the town in the nineteenth century by the Windsor family. Others included the Penarth Head Open Space, Plassey Square, Albert Square. The Shrubbery eventually lost its trees and shrubs, and from the 1920s was used as a car and lorry park. It was recently re-instated and officially opened by H.R.H. the Prince of Wales.

During the last decade of the nineteenth century and the first few years of the twentieth century, the Shrubbery was the site of one of the town's many al fresco gentlemen's urinals. In 1914 this was re-located across the road at the entrance to Dock Subway Road.

ARCOT STREET

This wide street of substantial Victorian stone houses was originally intended to be the town's main street[17], but the idea was overtaken by the rapid urbanisation that took place after the arrival of the railway in 1878. The name is a reminder of the victory won by Robert Clive (Clive of India) at the Battle of Arcot in Southern India in 1750.

The street was used as the route for the horse-buses operated by the Taff Vale Railway to convey passengers between their railway station and their hotel, the Penarth Hotel. It meant the steeper routes of Glebe Street and Albert Road could be avoided[18].

ARTILLERY HOUSE (LOST)

In the late 1840s a large mansion was built in the windswept isolation of Penarth Head. As a private residence it was known by at least two other names, Prospect House and Uppercliff. However, when the Penarth Head Fort and the Coastal Battery were built at the end of the 1890s, the house became the Officers' Quarters and its name was changed to Artillery House.

During the Second World War the fort and house were taken over by the American Armed Forces. Once the war had ended, the house fell into disrepair and suffered from acts of vandalism. It was eventually demolished to make way for a housing estate.

ARTILLERY QUARTERS (LOST)

The Glamorgan Artillery Barracks and Quarters were opened in the 1860s on a site bounded by what is today Harbour View Road, Plassey Square, High Street and the lane behind the Church in Wales School off Plassey Street. The original address was 9 Maughan Street. By 1892 the official address had changed to 32 High Street.

---

[17] E. T. Bevan, ibid.
[18] Mr Rowland: Notes on Old Penarth (unpublished).

The Quarters were used by various military groups - not only the Artillery, but also the Penarth Volunteer Rifle Corps and the Severn Sub-marine Miners. Following the building of the Woodland Place Drill Hall and the Penarth Head Fort, the Quarters were demolished and the site was built over at the turn of this century.

ASH PATH

In the 1700s a path used to run from Cornerswell Farm, across the fields to the Murch, and then on up to the village of Dinas Powys. A short section of this path remains and today joins St Cyres Road with Sully Road. This is known as the Ash Path.

AUGUSTA ROAD

The Earl of Plymouth, Robert Windsor Clive, married Alberta Paget in 1883. Her father was Sir Augustus Berkeley Paget, and her mother was Augusta Fane (Lady Boringdon), daughter of the 10th Earl of Westmorland.

BACK ROW

The first dwellings built in modern Cogan were a row of seven houses, which can still be seen at the western end of Cawmpore Street. They were built in the 1850s to house men working on the excavation of the Dock, and became known as Back Row. The original town plan shows that a grid of streets was to be built behind Back Row on land nearer what is today the Cowslip Estate. This plan was abandoned when the damming of Cogan Pill resulted in houses being able to be built closer to the Dock. Older citizens of Cogan still refer to the cottages as Back Row. I am indebted to ex-Councillor Harold Toye for this information. Oral tradition has it that a public house (now lost) used to operate at the end of Back Row, although no evidence has been found to substantiate this claim.

BALCONY VILLA

This large, charming house, which formed one of a pair along with Rock Villa, was built between 1861 and 1871 on the strand just above the level of High

ROCK VILLA AND BALCONY VILLA

The 'Villas' built c.1860's, demolished 1963.

Water Springs. The house was demolished in 1963 and a block of flats, Windsor Court, built on the site.

The house had a chequered career as a private residence and as a guest house. In 1876, for example, the Penarth Visitors List showed that a Mr and Mrs Davies of Clifton and the Misses Hunt were staying as paying guests.

In 1881 the occupant was E Stockdale, a Customs Official. Also in residence were his wife and a stepson, James Randell, plus three daughters, two sons and a nephew, along with a governess and general servants.

In 1886 it was the home of John Biggs and his family. Biggs was a brewer and owned one of Cardiff's many breweries, the South Wales Brewery, which stood between the Rhymney Railway and the Taff Vale Railway at its junction just north-west of Queen Street Station.

BALLAST WHARF (LOST)

In the nineteenth century between 80% and 90% of the vessels arriving at Penarth arrived in ballast. The local press in 1892 highlighted the fact that: "Of the large fleet of vessels crossing the Western Ocean in Ballast, Penarth had held by far the largest number on the West Coast of Britain"[19]. To remain manoeuvrable and to prevent capsizing, vessels, especially sailing ships, needed to be 'stiffened', by ballast, usually stone, although gravel, sand and sometimes even water was used. Before being able to load coal, the ballast had to be unloaded, sometimes into barges in the dock, but usually at the Ballast Wharf. The Wharf and Ballast Office stood on the bank of the River Ely just below what is today the site of the Tesco supermarket. Both the wharf and the office have now been lost, but at low water ballast stone can still be seen strewn along the river bank by the long shore drift. Today, however, it is mixed in with rubble dumped by modern builders.

Large quantities of ballast stone from all over the world was used for local building projects. Lord Bute even employed a full-time agent at Cardiff Docks to sell ballast stone to local builders[20]. The beautiful Ebenezer Chapel in Charles Street, Cardiff, is built entirely of ballast stone, and the two end houses in Bradford Place, Penarth, opposite Falconhurst, both have boundary walls made of ballast stone.

---

[19] Penarth Observer, 1892.
[20] J. Perkins, "Building Stones of Cardiff", 1984.

BALL HOUSE/POINT

Ball House is first recorded as Ball Rock Cottage in 1829 and stands on Ball Point, a promontory between St Mary's Well Bay and Sully Island. The name may be derived from bal(le), a Middle English word meaning a rounded hill or hillock. In the Ministerial Accounts to the Crown for the years 1433 to 1434, a reference is made to revenue from the foreshore fisheries around Penarth. The records also refer to produce being collected from the Balle Fishery. Both Ball House and Ball Point are clearly marked on early maps and charts[21]

BEACH BOATYARD (LOST)

The Penarth Promenade and Landing Pier Company Limited ran a popular and lucrative sideline to their major venture, the Penarth Pier. They hired a large number of small rowing boats and sailing dinghies, usually crewed by local men, and these can regularly be seen on old photographs[22]. A number of independent boat owners also worked off the beach. During the summer months the Pier Company's boats were moored on the foreshore, chained to the sea wall. Winter storage, maintenance and repairs were carried out in a small boat-yard at the foot of what are now the Windsor Court flats. The site of the yard was later used as an unofficial car park.

BEACH COTTAGE (LOST)

This substantial building, a large villa rather than a cottage, was one of the first buildings on Penarth's seafront, and was built in about 1860. By 1871 the house was occupied by Edward Morgan, his wife and family. Morgan owned and managed the numerous bathing machines that were hired out to modest Victorians. The bathing machines were stored in a large wooden building which used to stand on the site of what is today the Beach Shelter in the Italian Gardens.

Beach Cottage, which was located between Balcony and Rock Villas and the distinctive block of flats and cafes built in 1904 by Frederick Speed (today run as restaurants by the highly successful Rabiotti family), was demolished in the early 1960s to make way for the building of Windsor Court.

[21] Lieut. H. M. Denham, "Bristol Channel Survey, 1832".
[22] P. Carradice: "Beside the Seaside", 1992; D Ings: "Penarth in Old Picture Postcards", 1985; R. Thorne: "History of Penarth", Volumes 1 and 2 (1975 and 1976 respectively).

BEACH ROAD

This road, which includes a number of substantial Victorian houses, links the town centre with the seafront. When building work first commenced in the 1860s and 70s, the town's first major ship owner, James Ware, was one of the earliest residents. His house was known as Briarbank and the thoroughfare was known as Penarth Terrace.

BEACH WOOD (LOST)

This small dense wood was originally part of the grounds of Kymin House, but became separated from the house and grounds when Beach Road, which had originally run in front of the Park Superintendent's House, was re-routed along its present course in 1924.

The wood was an exciting playground for local children, and the diligent searcher used to be able to find an old well and a short section of a dried out water course, all that remained of the stream that used to run through the Kymin Dingle. In the undergrowth, meanwhile, a short section of the Old Beach Road could be seen. The area is now covered by the Seabank apartment block.

BEAUFORT CLUB (LOST)

We have already referred to the many drinking clubs that sprang up during the nineteenth century in Penarth's Docktown, and the Beaufort was one of them - notorious but short lived! During the 1860s and 70s the Beaufort Club occupied the premises that were later to become Huntley's General Store and Sub-Post Office in Maughan Street, now Queen's Road. The club only held a proper licence for a fewyears, although it continued to trade illegally for many more.

BEDWAS PLACE

Other, the Third Earl of Plymouth, (born 30 June 1707, died 23 November 1732), married Elizabeth, the daughter and heiress of Thomas Lewis of The Van, Caerphilly. Elizabeth inherited estates at Caerphilly, St Fagan's, Soberton in Hampshire and Bedwas. The only issue of the marriage was one son, Other, who was born in 1732 and who became the Fourth Earl of Plymouth.

BEECROFT

This large late Victorian town house, a classic of its genre, was built at the junction of Archer Road and Stanwell Road. The first occupant in the 1890s was Captain W E Raymond, Master Mariner. In 1899 the house became home to Captain James Jenkins, another Master Mariner, and his wife Catherine. By the 1920s they had moved to Cardiff whereupon they presented the house to the town.

Mrs Constance Maillard, one of the town's most celebrated citizens, worked tirelessly to establish a child care centre, and eventually in 1925 the town's first and much needed Maternity and Child Welfare Centre was opened. Its official title was "The Catherine Jenkins Institute Charity Trust". The centre was, and still is, remembered simply as 'Beecroft'.

The author clearly remembers going to Beecroft in the early years of the Second World War, its windows criss-crossed with wide sticky paper and protected by sand-bags. He has fond memories of the lovely rocking-horse!

BELLE VUE COTTAGE

The Cottage, in reality a large farmhouse, was demolished in 1883 and the town's Council Offices were built on the site. The building is now empty, as the Council Offices have moved to West House in Stanwell Road.

The Cottage was occupied in 1851 by one Evan Evans who is listed as a Farmer/Carpenter. Many of the farm holdings, including a market garden and a large orchard, were lost with the building of Salop Street, Salop Place and Bromfield Place. When a site was being cleared to build Albert Road School, a barn belonging to Belle Vue had to be demolished.

In 1861 the Cottage was listed as being the home of Frederick W Granger, Surgeon, and by 1871 it was occupied by Valentine Trayes. Trayes was a timber merchant and ship owner. In 1883, the occupier was Thomas Reeves and he ran the Windsor Nursery on the site.

BELGRAVIAN STORES (LOST)

This grandly named shop used to trade at Britannia Buildings, 15 Glebe Street, and was owned by Mrs Sully, who also owned the Roath Gymnasium in Cardiff. (The redoubtable Mrs Sully, by the way, was instrumental in breaking the male-only stranglehold on the Swimming Baths, but only in the face of strong opposition. She formed the first Ladies Swimming Club at the Penarth Baths in 1892.)

BERKELEY DRIVE

Other Archer, the Sixth Earl of Plymouth, died without issue on 10 July 1833, and the barony fell into abeyance. The first Earl of Plymouth (Second Creation) was Robert George Windsor Clive, who was born in 1857, and who was the grandson of Harriet, Other Archer's sister. Robert married Alberta Victoria Sarah Caroline Paget, daughter of Sir Augustus Berkeley Paget.

BETHANIA

The Welsh speaking Calvinistic Methodists split with their English speaking co-religionists in 1879, and left the Sardis Chapel, Plassey Street, where they had previously worshipped together. Having no permanent place of worship of their own they met at a number of venues, including a house in Ludlow Street, both Andrews' Large and Small Halls, and the Jubilee Hall. Dame Clara Novello Davies gave concerts at the Andrews' Hall and in the Jubilee Hall on at least on two occasions to raise money towards the building of a permanent home for the Calvinistic Methodists. When sufficient funds were raised a charming little Chapel, Bethania, was built in Hickman Road in the 1890s. Unfortunately this little 'gem', like so many of Penarth's historic buildings, has recently and needlessly been demolished, the site now boarded off and empty - another blot on the Penarth landscape.

BEVAN'S ROW (LOST)

Thomas Bevan was a prominent citizen of Penarth in the nineteenth century. A builder of repute, he was a non-conformist in both political and religious terms. He was one of the many men who emerged to challenge the Windsor/ Clive's High Church and High Tory control of the town. Bevan was a long term member of the Local Board, the forerunner of the much-lamented Penarth Urban District Council.

Bevan built and lived in the large house known as Pembroke Cottage that still stands today at the junction of Albert Road and Salop Street. Among the many properties he built was a lovely terrace of small red-brick houses in the

Bethania Welsh Calvinistic Methodist Chapel now unfortunately demolished.

1890s and originally named after the builder himself. The houses, now part of Lavernock Road, run from Hazel Road towards Powys Road.

BILLYBANKS

This appellation was and still is used to refer to the large open area, now partly built on, that turns westward from the Royal Hotel along the northern edge of Penarth Ridge, and below the old Catholic Church, Harbour View Road, and Plassey Square. Before urbanization began in the 1850s, the area had been used for grazing, and at various times surface quarrying had taken place in the area. We know this was certainly the case during the Roman occupation between AD 55 - AD 400.

Before the building of the dock and urbanization the area had been bisected by a vigorous stream which cut through the ridge, the break in the ridge, and the escarpment. The remains of the once fast flowing stream can still be seen, although the volume of water in it has been diminished by a combination of drainage and culverting. The stream used to join a pill that cut through a shingle beach, but both were lost with the excavation of the Dock.

During the 1860s and 70s quarrying took place along the northern escarpment of the Penarth Ridge and there were five quarries within the Billybanks perimeter. One of these was located directly beneath the old Catholic Church (these days a housing estate), and was the largest and deepest quarry in the town. There were also lime-pits and lime-kilns, and to serve these units and the adjacent quarries, sidings were run in from the High Level Sidings. The official TVR title for the sidings was William's Sidings.

The spoil from the various workings were tipped from a complex network of tramways, and as these spoil heaps grew they came to be called "mountains" by the local Bowery Boys. The largest was known as Spion Kop. The spoil heaps wereused to great effect as playgrounds for the local scallywags. Spoil heaps are known in most industrial areas, including the South Wales Valleys, as "banks"[23], so it is safe to assume that the derivation of Billybanks is a diminution of William's (as in the sidings) to Billie's and the addition of banks, hence Billybanks.

A popular theory regarding the derivation of Billybanks is that the quarry manager was one Billy Banks, although no evidence has yet been found to

---

[23] I am indebted to Cllr. Janice Birch for this information.

prove this. In more recent times, the area, especially that covered by the Prince Charles Courts, etc, was known as Salter's Fields.

BIJOU

The Bijou, or to give it its full title the Penarth Pier Bijou Pavilion, was a large wooden concert hall erected at the seaward end of the pier in 1907. Oscar Mills, an erstwhile dancer-cum-comedian, was its first manager, having leased the hall from the Pier Company. Before 1907 all the entertainments held on the Pier, the revues, the ball evenings, etc. were held al fresco, although if the weather was inclement large temporary canvas awnings would be erected. The Bijou was destroyed by fire on Monday, 3 August 1931.

BIRDCAGE

The Clive Arms, John Street, was one of the town's first public houses, having been built around the 1850s in the middle of a row of cottages. In the decade at least ten, and perhaps as many as twelve, other public houses were built to serve the growing population. Because of its minuscule size the pub has been known affectionately to generations of Penarth tipplers and topers as the Birdcage. It is certainly the town's smallest pub and the only one not sited on a street corner. It was also the town's last cider-house. Even with modernisation and a little enlargement, it still retains its local warmth.

The first landlord of the Clive Arms was George Lewis, and by the time of the 1871 Census the landlord was a Mr W. Sadler. Close neighbours were Matthew Frost, a ferryman, D. Denman, a Channel pilot, Chas Tree, a sailmaker, and Richard Vizard, an omnibus driver, who no doubt drove one of Soloman Andrews's horse buses.

BLACK BENCH (LOST)

The name Black Bench enjoyed common currency up until the last decades of the 19th century, especially among men employed in the coastal maritime trades such as Channel pilots, hobblers, tug boatmen, Severn trow men etc. It applied to the extensive outcrop of hard rock that runs seawards from under the Penarth Head. It was used by mariners as a tidal marker.

Seen from above or from the Channel, the thick seaweed cover gives the impression that the rocks are indeed black. The outcrop is almost uniformly raised above the foreshore pebbles and shingle, and from a distance it looks as if it has a flat top, hence the reference to bench. From roughly 1900 onwards it became known by the name of the Black Rocks.

The extensive outcrop was a constant hazard to shipping, especially in the days of sail, as small vessels crept in at half-water. The advent of radar and the provision of the Penarth Head Buoy, have lessened the dangers. Captain Smyth noted that the "... Black Bench was ... a well-known projection under Penarth Head, emphatically called the Black Bench, especially when the easterlies were blowing[24]."

BLACK HAYS (lost)

In 1766 the Black Hays was described as nine acres of mead and woodland. It used to form part of the West House Farm, which was owned by Catherine Edwards, and covered an area fronting onto what is today West House and stretching down towards Victoria Square.

BLACK TANK

The Black Tank was a large and deep cast iron reservoir raised high on a substantial brick base, its function being to hold water for the Penarth Dock Locomotive Sheds. The sheds were built at the western (Cogan) end of the Penarth Ridge, where Tesco's car park stands today. The Black Tank was constructed high on the ridge behind and above the sheds. It was scrapped in the late 1950s, although the remains of its extensive brick base can still be seen at the end of the footpath that runs westward from High View Road.

Before it was demolished, the tank was used by the local Bowery Boys as a "swimming pool", especially when the tide was out or when the presence of the Docks Police prevented them from using the Dock. In order to gain access to the tank, you had to climb the brick base and then scale the precipitous sides of the tank itself, and to achieve this was seen as one of the local "initiation rites". The boys trying to get up to the top of the tank would be showered with cascades of water and verbally taunted by those of their peers already cavorting in the water.

The tank was a wonderful place, and swimming in that elevated pool, high on the sun-drenched ridge, was like swimming in the sky.

---

[24] W. H. Smythe: Nautical observations on the port and maritime vicinity of Cardiff, 1840.

BLEAK HOUSE (LOST)

The Chief Coastguard traditionally lived in the house at the seaward end of the row of Coastguard cottages that run down Tower Hill from Plymouth Road to Marine Parade. Its official name was Bleak House. The first occupant was James B. Bryan, Chief Officer, who was one of the men instrumental in getting the Royal National Lifeboat Institution to station a lifeboat at Penarth in 1863. When the Coastguard cottages were built a year later in 1864 they stood in splendid isolation, so the house was aptly named.

BOARD SCHOOL

The town's Board School in Albert Road was opened on 18 September 1876. The Penarth School Board had been set up in 1874 and its members were all well-known local businessmen, including John Batchelor, who was its first Chairman. Other members were A. Arundel, A. Dalziel, James Edwards (of the Taff Vale Railway), and E. Vachell. Two sites were originally considered for the Board School. One option was to adapt the school rooms already in existence in Wesley Lane (now Chapel Lane), premises that belonged to the Wesleyan Chapel (now St. Pauls). The other was to put the school on the corner of Salop Street and Parish Road (now Albert Road and the site of Mr Bevan's house - see Bevan's Row). Both sites, however, were finally rejected as being unsuitable and the school was instead built on former glebeland at the top of Parish Road.

The first buildings were opened in 1876 and extensions were added in 1883 and 1886. The beautiful little Head Teacher's House can still be seen between what used to be the Boys' School (on the north side) and the Girls' School (to the south). The house is now the home of the School Caretaker.

The school was designed by Henry C. Harris in the Gothic style. Harris also co-designed the Penarth Public Swimming Baths on the Esplanade.

BOWERY

The original Docktown, built during the 1850s and 60s, covered an area bounded by Maughan Street (now High Street) to the west, Parish Road (now Albert Road) to the east, Windsor Road to the south, and the Dock escarpment to the north. This area was, and still is, affectionately known, especially to those born within its confines, as the Bowery. Penarthians born in the area but

The Board School, Albert Road School, opened September, 1876.

who subsequently move away take great pride in claiming the status of a Bowery Boy or Girl. None more so than one of the town's best known politicians, Cllr. John L. Flanigan.

The derivation of the name is unclear, as is the period in which it was first used. Two theories, however, have been advanced, both of which have a degree of credence. In the 19th century, seamen returning from New York, America's major sea port at the time, men who would have drunk and caroused in the famous Bowery district in that city, might have seen some parallels with the Penarth Docktown, with its seamen's boarding houses, public houses, drinking clubs, shebeens and brothels.

Another theory is that many Irish families in their desperation to escape English rule and the potato famines left Ireland for America. Some would have taken up lodgings in the poor areas of New York, such as the Bowery. Many re-crossed the Atlantic and came to South Wales. There was plentiful work in this part of the country - many new docks were being constructed at this time and there was work to be had sinking mine shafts. Many such people came to Penarth. Indeed the author has friends from two different families whose ancestors raised siblings who had been born in Ireland, America and Penarth.

A classic example of this can be found in the Census of 1861[25]. John Hurley, his wife and children were living in one of the town's first houses built specifically to provide accommodation for men excavating the dock, this one in Glebe Street. The Census shows that one son and a daughter had been born in Ireland, two sons and a daughter had been born in the USA, and one son had been born in Penarth. There was also a lodger in the house, a fellow Irishman, who like Hurley worked as an excavator on the Dock. The Hurleyfamily and others like them could well have brought the name Bowery back with them from downtown New York.

No note on the Bowery would be complete without mentioning perhaps the most famous Bowery Boy of all, the late, much lamented 'Captain Silva', who always took every opportunity and great pleasure in boasting of his Bowery pedigree.

BRADENHAM PLACE

In 1523 the Duke of Suffolk was sent at the head of an English army to invade France, and Sir Andrew de Windsor, Baron Windsor, son of Thomas de

[25] E. A. Benjamin: Penarth 1841-71. (1980).

Windsor, Lord Stanwell, accompanied him as one of his principal commanders. His military services were recognized by the King, and in 1529 Andrew was elevated to the peerage and by letters patent created Baron Windsor of Bradenham in the county of Buckingham. The estates at Bradenham had been an ancient seat of the de Windsors since 1198.

Between 1825 and 1848 this same Bradenham was the home of Isaac Disraeli, the father of Benjamin, later Lord Beaconsfield. After his father's death in 1848, Benjamin Disraeli occupied the mansion for a short time between 1848 and 1850.

BRADEN RELICE/REOLICE (LOST)

The Anglo-Saxon Chronicles contain numerous references to Braden Relice, one of the early names for the Flat Holm. Braden is an Old English word meaning broad, while Relice is derived from the Old Irish, relig, which can be translated both as graveyard and/or relics from the Latin reliquiae. Both Flat Holm and Steep Holm were used as burial places, and many graves have been found on both islands[26].

BRADFORD PLACE

The Second Earl of Bradford was the father of Lady Mary Selina Bridgeman, who married Robert Clive on 20 October 1852. There were four children from the marriage, Robert George, Georgina Harriet Charlotte, Henrietta Lucy, and Mary Agnes.

BREWERY

Brewery is the name given to two sites in Penarth. One the Windsor Brewery, or to give it its full title Lovett's Windsor Steam Brewery, can still be seen immediately behind the Windsor Hotel. It was only recently renamed the Tut & Shive. The building has had a new facade built out of local brick, although the rest of the building is in the original locally-quarried stone, as too is part of the original front boundary wall.

The Windsor Hotel is one of the town's original public houses, the pub and brewery being opened in 1856. At that time both were owned and managed by

---

[26] D. R. Paterson: Early Cardiff Placenames. 1926.

Henry Lovett and his son, Frederick. Frederick Lovett was also the agent for the Inman Line who operated steamers during the 1870s and 80s. When the hotel and brewery opened, they stood at the junction of Windsor Road and Maughan Street, which subsequently became High Street. An early advertisement boasted it was "the only brewery in the town" and that their "celebrated home brewed beer was made solely from pure spring water, malt and hops". It was provided in "casks [of] 4½, 9, 18, 36 and 54 gallons".

The other 'brewery' was in fact the Penarth Mineral Water Factory, the yard and buildings of which can still be seen in the middle of Bromfield Place. During the 19th century the owner was a Mr Watson who lived in the house next to the 'brewery' at number 13. In the garden of number 13 there is a capped well that was used to provide water to the business being operated next door. Until Bromfield Place was built in the 1880s, the site was the orchard for Belle Vue Cottage. Mr Watson, incidentally, also owned the Cardiff Aerated Water Company Limited in Spring Gardens, Roath.

BRIARBANK

This imposing house, built on a steep, south-facing bank and with extensive gardens, overlooks Beach Road, formerly Penarth Terrace, and enjoys panoramic views over the Bristol Channel. Briarbank, which was built during the 1860s, was the first house in Beach Road. All the others in the road are built on what had used to be the Briar Bank[27].

The first owner of Briarbank was James Ware, who was born in Bridgwater. The son of the Dock master there, he went to sea at an early age but came to Penarth and settled in the town in the early 1860s. He was the town's first major ship owner, a Justice of the Peace, and a member of the Local Board.

Ware's large schooner-rigged steam yacht, the Carrina was the second vessel to enter the new Barry Dock when it was opened on 18 July 1889. The first had been the S.S. Arno out of Sunderland, and the Carrina had been followed by the local tug, the Falcon.

BRICK PONDS (LOST)

The town's first brickworks, the Cogan Pill Tile and Brick Company, was established in the early 1860s. The extensive ovens, associated buildings and

[27]   Mr Rowlands, ibid.

workings stood where the Leisure Centre is today. Before this, clay had been taken from the area for small-scale brick making. The houses of the original Dock town were built of local stone during the 1850s and 60s. The second and third phases, which went up in the 1860s and 70s and 1870s and 80s respectively, were mainly built using bricks from the Cogan Brickworks and local stone.

The excavation of clay on such a large scale left numerous holes which quickly filled with land drainage, rain water and tidal water from the River Ely. These "brick ponds" became a constant source of problems as the water became stagnant and local people dumped household refuse in them. They eventually attracted a great deal of public and official criticism, with the local press reporting in 1892 that "A whole army of doctors [seven in fact, when the population of Cogan was just 1,600] were seen in Cogan last week. It appears there was a serious outbreak of scarlatina (or scarlet fever), more than 30 families were afflicted. Have those miserable receptacles of stagnant water anything to do with it?". The article continued "They have been condemned time after time, they should be filled in and drained off to make them innocuous"[28].

On 28 September 1892, the Local Board discussed a letter from Mr Downing, mortgagee of the Cogan Pill Tile and Brickworks, who wrote declining "to spend a penny in abating the nuisance caused by the brick ponds". He suggested that the topsoil and spoil from the building of the new road from Cogan to the Merry Harrier could be used to fill in the ponds. A record of a meeting of the Penarth Urban District Council held on 30 April, 1901 which appeared in the PenarthObserver noted : "Mr Smith urged attention to the Brickponds [which had been] giving off a disagreeable smell. The Clerk will see Mr Corbett.[29]"

The numerous brick ponds were eventually filled in during the first decades of this century, except for the one that remains today and which is known locally as the Duckpond. The brickworks themselves closed in the 1890s.

BRIDGEMAN ROAD

This road is named after Lady Selina Bridgeman, daughter of the Earl of Bradford, who married Robert Clive on 20 October 1852. An early resident of

---

[28]   Penarth Observer, 1892.
[29]   Penarth Observer, 1901.

the road was J. P. Jones, who built and lived at Ashdene. He was the builder and architect responsible for seeing many of Soloman Andrew's major projects to fruition in Cardiff and Penarth. Among other buildings, J. P. Jones designed Cardiff Central Market.

BRISTOL CHANNEL

It is impossible to establish precisely where the Bristol Channel starts and finishes, and what area it covers. One definition is that the Channel stretches from King Road at the mouth of the River Avon, down as far as Lundy Island. An early name for this area was the Severn Sea. As Bristol developed into England's second busiest port during the 14th and 15th centuries, however, and trade with France increased, we find evidence that the name began to change. One of the earliest written references to it appears in Leyden's famous sea atlas published in the middle of the sixteenth century. This shows it as "De Canel van Brosh". An earlier fifteenth century French chart had called it "Le Canal de Bristol" while a later French chart, produced by H. Jaillot in 1693, shows it as the "Canal de Bristol". The name was subsequently anglicised to the Bristol Channel, the name it is still known by today.

BRITANNIA BUILDINGS

The original buildings in Glebe Street, between Ludlow Street and Plassey Street, were built in the 1860s. At the Ludlow Street end, then numbered 6 (approximately where Chris Capus has his shop today) there could be found the notorious drinking den known as the Clifton Club. The row of buildings at the Plassey Street end also included the town's first Fire Engine Station, which had been built circa 1875, as well as the first Reading Room (again circa 1875).

These original buildings were demolished in 1901 and rebuilt as the Britannia Buildings (see Belgravian Store). The occupant of number 4 was Joseph Broadfoot who just happened to be a shoe and boot-maker.

BRODEFORD (LE) (LOST)

During the eighth and ninth centuries, Viking raids became increasingly savage and prolonged. The Anglo-Saxon Chronicle tells us that Vikings, under two Jarls, Othor and Harald, sailed up the Severn Sea and raided both shores.

Llandaff was attacked twice, first in 894 AD and again in 915 AD. The Vikings also settled and traded and some fought as mercenaries for various Welsh princes. Womanby Street, Cardiff, is a reminder of these days, being derived from the Old Norse hundemanby, which translates as the "stranger's quarter"[30].

An ecclesiastical document dated 1433 refers to a fishery in the sea off Penarth called "Le Brodefjord" This is a derivation from the Norse fiord/fjord which means a long narrow inlet, and brode, or broad, which would graphically describe the wide stretch of water between Lavernock Point and the Penarth Head that runs between the Penarth foreshore and the parallel sandbanks. Directly across the Bristol Channel there is a sandbank known as Langford Grounds, a derivation of Long Fjord[31].

In Minister's Accounts to Henry VI, the Brodeford is described as "a fishery belonging to the Manor of Cosmeston". It goes on to report the revenue from the various fisheries: "2/5 (approximately 12 new pence) for fisheries Reves, Balle, and for a fishery at Pennarth in the sea called Le Brodeford 1/4" (approximately 7 new pence). The exact location of the Reve has not yet been established, although the Balle could well be the area off what is today known as Ball Point, Lavernock.

This same account also records that "... nothing [was received] for the sale of plasterstone, none being sold" -a reference to the sale of what may well have been alabaster. If this is the case, it is the earliest reference to the sale of alabaster from the Penarth foreshore.

BRODESLYME (LE) (LOST)

Various documents dating from the fourteenth and fifteenth centuries mention Le Brodeslyme, the vast expanse of mud and slime between Cardiff and Penarth. References can also be found in earlier ecclesiastical charters to fishing rights in the area and others relating to the land surrounding the mud flats. In the early days of the Norman occupation, numerous gifts of land were made to local religious orders. Gilbert de Constantin and Gilbert de Clare gifted areas of the Brodeslyme and surrounding lands during the twelfth and thirteenth centuries. The monks of Margam Abbey built the grange farm that was originally known as the Abbot's Grange, a fifteenth century farm that still

[30] D. R. Paterson: "Early Cardiff: a short account of its street names", 1926.
[31] G Farr: "Somerset Harbours", 1954.

stands on the site of the junction of Clive Street and Stockland Street in Grangetown. The Abbot of St. Augustines gave the monks of Margam "50 acres in Pennarth and Costenton (Cosmeston) in the moor next to Kerdif between the water of Taff and water of Ely for 45 marks beforehand.[32]"

BROMFIELD PLACE

One of the numerous street names derived from the Windsor/Clive/Plymouth dynasty. Bromfield was an estate in Salop owned by the Clive family.

BURTON & HOOPERS (LOST)

During the nineteenth century, and especially during the last two decades as the New Town south of Windsor Road developed, Penarth was home to a myriad of small private schools. The school run by Messrs. Burton and Hooper was an exception in that it was established during the late 1870s at 72[33], Maughan Street (now Queen's Road). It continued in operation until the early 1880s[34]. Its siting in the very middle of Daggertown perhaps helps explain the schools' brief existence!

BUTE COTTAGE

E. T. Bevan states that ancestors of his, Thomas and Mary Evans[35], died of cholera in 1854 within days of each other, and claims that Thomas Evans actually built Bute Cottage.

The 1841 Census shows Bute Villa (Cottage) as being occupied by Thomas Evans, a pilot, and indeed the 1851 Census still has Evans down as the occupant, although by that time his occupation was given as a farmer.

Thomas and Mary Evans, aged 47 and 48 years of age respectively, were buried at St. Augustine's churchyard on 5 September 1854. If Thomas Evans did build Bute Cottage he must have done so around 1830. In 1855 the occupant is shown as William Richards.

When it was first built the Cottage was in the Parish of Cogan, which was owned by the Bute family. In 1766, John Mountstuart, Lord of Bute, married

[32] Paterson, ibid.
[33] Old numbering.
[34] Slater's Directory, 1885.
[35] E. T. Bevan, ibid.

Charlotte Jane, daughter of the Viscount of Windsor, and on her father's death Charlotte inherited Cardiff Castle and its estates, including the parishes of Roath, Llanishen, Llandaff and Lavernock. On Charlotte's death in 1800, the Castle and estates passed to Bute, who twelve days after his wife's internment in the Parish Church at Roath married Fanny, daughter of the wealthy banker, Thomas Coutts. In 1793, Bute had bought up the estates of Calvert Richard Jones. These included the manors of Kibbor, Cogan and Leckwith, the advowsons (i.e. the rights of patronage to a church benefice) of Llandough, Cogan and Leckwith, as well as several farms, including properties at Cogan, Roath and at Henstaff in the Vale of Glamorgan[36].

The lane that runs alongside the Cottage follows the route of an ancient footpath that used to lead from the Parish Road across fields to where West Terrace stands today, before turning northwards across fields up to the Glebelands.

CABMAN'S SHELTER

This unique and beautifully designed shelter was built in the early 1880s directly outside Penarth Town Station as a refuge for the local cab men. The building costs were met by a group of local dignitaries. It was here the cab men with their hansom cabs waited to ply for hire.

In 1892 following numerous complaints in the local press and to the Local Board regarding both the external and the internal condition of the shelter, the cab men, led by a Mr White, agreed to clean and maintain it on a rota system. However, the Penarth Observer reported on 1 June 1901 that: "Mr S.A. Brain [the famous brewer, who lived just across the way at Roxburgh] complained of an offensive smell coming from the Station Cab stand ... he suggested it should be washed down every day." Mr Brain was later informed that the area was hosed down every morning at 5.30 a.m.

In 1890 licensed cab men included Messrs. Bright, Critchett, Hooper, James, Pawley, Warren, Webber and no fewer than four gentlemen named White.

The shelter, like so many of the little gems of Penarth's architectural heritage, was wantonly demolished.

---

[36] John Davies: Cardiff and the Marquesses of Bute (1981).

CAMARAT

This beautiful house, now known as Park Mount, was built during the late 1930s and at one time stood in extensive landscaped gardens (now a block of flats) overlooking Alexandra Park. The house was built for Mr C. Howell, a well-known sportsman, sports administrator, businessman and shipowner.

During the Spanish Civil War, Howell's vessels ran General Franco's blockade, and one of them, the 'Jeanne M', was bombed on 29 May 1938 by Franco's German allies as it lay alongside in Barcelona Docks. The vessel was subsequently repaired at Barry Dock[1].

CAPE HORN

The name Cape Horn is not heard very often today except among older residents of the Bowery district of the town. It is used to describe the corner occupied by the RoyalHotel, one of the town's original public houses. Anyone who has tried to round this corner between Queen's Road and Arcot Street when a south-westerly gale is blowing will be only too aware of why the town's old "shell-backs", veterans of voyages to the southernmost tip of South America, dubbed it Cape Horn.

CATHOLIC CHURCH AND SCHOOL

The growth of industry in South Wales during the 19th century, and especially the Dock building programme, saw the influx of many people from Ireland, especially from the south-east area around Cork. The majority came to escape the potato famines and arrived in South Wales as "human ballast" in returning empty coal vessels. This was, of course, illegal, and the pitiful immigrants were landed on the Penarth foreshore or the mud flats of Penarth Harbour.

From 1860 Father Stephen Bruno of the Fathers of Charity had celebrated Mass in various places, including rooms above the shop now known as Table Talk on the corner of Glebe Street. He also preached in a number of stable lofts in Wesley Lane, including those still in existence behind the Royal Hotel, and in the 'Haunted House' on the corner of Salop Street and High Street.

In 1863 Father Fortunatus Signini approached Lady Plymouth with a request for a donation of land on which the Roman Catholic Church could build a place of worship. The following year, Father L. Nedelec gave an open air Mass to

---

[37]   P. M. Heaton: Welsh Blockade Runners in the Spanish Civil War. (1985).

about 600 men working on the dock construction. In 1876 Fr. Bruno bought a tract of land at the top of Arcot Street and High Street, and a Church, Presbytery and School were built. They were opened by the Right Reverend Bishop Hetley on 11 April 1877, and the first Parish Priest was Father Clarke[2].

A larger church, St. Joseph's, was built in Wordsworth Avenue in 1914, and in 1970 a much needed school was built on the Sully Road. The original buildings have recently been restored and converted into private dwellings.

In 1863, Fr Bruno had been priest at St. Peter's Catholic Church in Tredegarville, while Fr Nedelec was the priest at St. David's Church, David Street[39].

CATTLE PENS (LOST)

The remains of the town's cattle pens can be seen to the right of the entrance to Gimber's Garage complex just off Station Approach. The remains show an extensive raised platform built of local stone and yellow brick, capped with large slabs of the ubiquitous Radyr Redstone. The pens were serviced by two short railway lines running from the main line.

In the third week of May 1892, the local Magistrate's Court, with J.S. Corbett (Cogan Pill House), J.P. Thompson (Redlands, later re-named Roxburgh), and Valentine Trayes (Northcliffe) sitting as magistrates, heard a case against Richard Guy, a well known businessman and butcher of Clive Place, who was accused of taking 33 pigs from the animal pens. Similar cases against Shadrack Smith of Cliff Street, and Henry Venning of High Street were also heard. They were all charged with removing cows and calves from the pens, all charges contrary to the Contagious Diseases (Animals) Act of 1878. Guy defended himself and was found not guilty on a technicality[40]. As a result, the charges against Smith and Venning were also dropped. One of Mr Guy's sons was the late Dr. Guy of Hickman Road.

CAROLINE PLACE (LOST)

When the houses in what is today Rosebery Place were first built, they were known as Caroline Place. In June 1897 Mr Tape (who in 1897 was living at The

[38] D. Fanning: St. Joseph's, Penarth (1990).
[39] Wakeford's Cardiff Directory, 1863.
[40] Penarth Observer, 1892.

Elms, Windsor Road) submitted plans to the Penarth Urban District Council to build five villas in Caroline Place. By 1900 it had been renamed Rosebery Place. One of the first occupants was Mr Percy Cadle, a well-known Cardiff tobacconist.

Rosebery was a Victorian statesman and in 1894, the year in which he became Prime Minister, the Marquis of Bute held a sumptious dinner for him. Following the death of the Marquis, Rosebery paid a touching tribute to him at a meeting of the Scottish History Society. Lord Rosebery, the fifth earl, was formerly Archibald Primrose.

CAWMPORE STREET

The first dwellings to be built in what is now Cawmpore Street were the seven small houses built at the western end. These were erected in the 1850s, at which time they were known as Back Row and subsequently Cogan Row. During the 1900s four or five larger villas were built at the eastern (Pill Street) end, including Glanystwyth and Greendyke, and these were officially in Cawmpore Road. By 1912 there were 12 villas in the road and the Row still stood in isolation. By 1915 yet more villas had been built and the road had been united with Back Row to become Cawmpore Street. The row of houses opposite the Row were built in the 1920s.

The name is a reminder of a bloody massacre that took place during the Indian Mutiny in 1857.

CEFN-Y-WRACH

This extensive gravel-strewn bank that was to be found on top of a bed of marl, lay off Penarth Head and separated the mouth of the rivers Ely and Taff. Until it was dredged in the middle of the last century, the bank used to dry out at low water and was a navigational hazard at high tide.

The Welsh name, which translates as Witch's Back, is a corruption of the Old Norse rak. The word 'rack' was commonly used in association with fjords and is best translated as "something swirled up by the action of wind and water"[41]. This aptly describes the tidal movement over a gravel bank,

---

[41]   D R Paterson: "Early Cardiff: a short account of its street names and surrounding place names". 1926.

especially with a prevailing westerly wind blowing straight down the River Ely.

CENTRAL CLUB (LOST)

In the 19th century this drinking club occupied the large house that stands at the bottom of Ferry Lane at its junction with Paget Terrace. An early manager was Chas. Isgar.

CHANTRY RISE

This name commemorates a chantry that is reputed to have stood roughly between what is today Britten Road and Castle Avenue. G. O. Pierce[42] writes that "(I)n the parish [of Penarth] is a ruin, now converted into a barn, which was formerly a chantry chapel, probably connected with or served by the monks of the monastery of 'Llandough-super-Ely'". Old ecclesiastical buildings, being robustly built and designed to last a long time, were commonly used as farms -compare here the Abbey at Woodspring directly across the Bristol Channel from Penarth.

We know there was a farm on the site by 1700, the Cwrt-y-Vil Farm, and the remains of old buildings can be found in the gardens of houses in the area.

CHAPEL LANE

A T-shaped lane linking Arcot Street, Glebe Street and Salop Street, Chapel Lane has numerous old stables as well as the buildings that used to house one of the town's leading bakers, the Cross Family Bakery. When it was first built the lane was called Wesley Lane. The houses in Glebe Street that back onto the Lane were bought when they were first built in the 1850s by an organization called The Llantrisant Club.

CHARLOTTE STREET

As with so many of the street names in both Cogan and Penarth, this again evokes the town's Windsor/Clive/Plymouth connection. Georgina Harriet Charlotte, born 1858, was the eldest daughter of Robert Clive, the Member of

---

[42] G O Pierce: "Place Names of the Dinas Powis Hundred", 1968.

Parliament for Ludlow, and Lady Selina Bridgeman. An earlier Charlotte was Charlotte Herbert, whose first husband was Lord John Jefferies, son of the infamous Judge Jefferies, otherwise known as the Hanging Judge. When John died in 1702, Charlotte married Thomas, Viscount Windsor, who had served with distinction as a soldier under the Duke of Marlborough. The Herberts built Cogan Pill House.

CHARTERIS CLOSE

Ivor Miles, the Second Earl of Plymouth, married Lady Irene Charteris. Ivor, who died in 1943, was the second son of Robert Windsor-Clive, Earl of Plymouth, Baron Windsor, and his wife Alberta Paget. Ivor's eldest brother, Other, died in 1908 and a third brother, Archer, was killed in action in 1914.

CHERWELL ROAD

The Cherwell is a tributary of the River Thames and flows through the Windsor's Stanwell Estates in Berkshire. Walter de Windsor was Lord Stanwell in the 12th century.

CHRISTCHURCH

The first record of Congregationalists holding a religious service in Penarth is in 1845. The service was held at John Taylor's farm, which stood on roughly the site of the present National Westminster Bank. The service was conducted by John Thomas, a lay preacher, and the congregation was made up of Welsh Congregationalists, who were also known as the Independents.

The first record of English Congregationalists is a service held in 1882 in Andrews's Small Hall, the Lesser Hall, in Ludlow Lane. Later services were held in Andrews'sLarge Hall, Albert Road. In 1883 the English Congregationalists erected a large iron church on the corner of Windsor Road and Railway Terrace. This was later to be used as a public hall, a Drill Hall and a cinema.

In 1894, the Congregationalists built an outstanding Gothic-style church, Christchurch, on a site in Stanwell Road that had been offered by Solomon Andrews in exchange for the iron church and site. Andrews also donated £50 towards the building costs. The church, a landmark with its elegant 110 feet

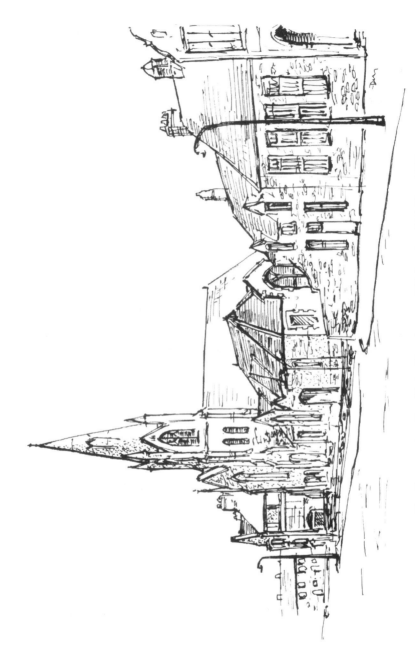

The Congregationalists Christ Church, opened Wednesday, 11th May, 1897.

spire, was opened on Wednesday, 11 May 1897 when the Reverend Horton, a former president of the Congregational Union, preached to over 600 people. The church was designed by Habershon and Fauckner of Newport. The cost of the site and the building totalled £6,500.

Joseph Parry and his family, who lived in Plymouth Road, then Victoria Road, between 1888 and 1903, were members of Christchurch and Parry played the organ in both the iron church and the new church. There is a record of his playing during the first week of March 1892 when "a sacred concert was performed at Christchurch Congregational Chapel in Windsor Road under Dr. Parry"[43].

Sadly, the church has now been demolished, although the local Scouts Association, through the efforts of Gilbert Long, saved some of the original stonework and used it to build a large fire place in their new Scouts Headquarters.

CHURCH TERRACE

This charming row of houses, built using bricks manufactured by the Penarth Brickworks, Windsor Road, originally stood in Maughan Street, now Queen's Road. They were built on the site of an earlier large Anglican iron church (St. Paul's) which had been erected in the 1890s and demolished in 1906, when it was sold and re-erected as St. Barruc's on Barry Island. A commemorative plaque, set high on the wall of one of the houses, dates them from 1909.

CINEMA PALACE (LOST)

The Cinema Palace was one of the town's first cinemas, being opened by Mr White at the end of 1911 at 19 Glebe Street. It is now the part of Social Club.

CINEMA THEATRE (LOST)

The Penarth Times of 7 January 1937 states that "Penarth's first cinema was opened by the Willmore Brothers in 1910 at number 21 Glebe Street". As was the case with the Cinema Palace, the Cinema Theatre operated from a converted shop. The Cinema Theatre was able to hold an audience of 120 and

---

43 Penarth Observer, March 1892.

the projector was hand-cranked. By 1916 the premises had become the headquarters of the Penarth Volunteer Rifle Corps.

CLARENCE TERRACE

This terrace at the bottom of Plassey Street comprises a row of red brick houses built into the southern edge of the Penarth Ridge. Every house is entered by a steep flight of stone steps. Built in 1892, they stand directly opposite the cottages in Norris Row. The houses built in New Plassey Street (also called Lower Plassey Street), which ran between High Street and Clarence Terrace and Norris Row went up between 1888 and 1891. They were all incorporated with Plassey Street in 1892 when a renumbering exercise was carried out. A name and date plaque can be seen at the Cogan end of the terrace.

CLIFFSIDE

Penarth was justifiably renowned for the large and handsome mansions built and owned by its ship-owning families, most of whom moved into Penarth after the opening of the Penarth Extension Railway in 1878.

Unfortunately these architectural gems, each one individually designed and standing in extensive landscaped gardens, safe behind massive boundary walls, have all now disappeared. The last to be built was Cliffside, which was constructed in 1919 at the seaward end of Forrest Road and only recently demolished to provide the site of a housing estate called The Paddocks. All that remains is the beautiful boundary wall built out of local lias stone and a few of the trees that used to form the grand avenue between the original paddocks, the large detached stables and the house itself.

The house was built for the enigmatic ship and coal-mine owner Sir Sven Wohlford Hansen who was born in Cardiff in 1876, the son of a Norwegian immigrant, Carl Hansen. As well as owning a large fleet of merchant ships, he purchased Edward Nicholls's entire fleet, the Hall Line, plus four vessels from Pyman, Watson & Co. He also owned the Graham's Navigation Colliery at Tredegar, as well as the Clearhouses Shipbuilding Yard near Bideford, Devon. He was the only South Wales shipowner to own ketch-rigged sailing barges, which were ideal for making local coastal deliveries of coal. His Haig Shipping Company owned two such barges, the Diana, built at Rye in 1891, and the Mountsfield, also builtat Rye in 1890. Like so many of his fellow shipowners in the area, he owned a large yacht, the Nicholson-built schooner Adela.[44]

[44]   C. M. Tarver: "Penarth Yacht Club, 1880-1980" (1980).

CLIFF VILLA (LOST)

Cliff Villa was the original, albeit short-lived, name given to the imposing mansion built in the 1840s on the cliff edge overlooking the mouth of the River Ely, and these days better known as Northcliff. The 1851 Census shows that Mr H. H. Parry, a retired shipping agent, his wife, and two servants were in residence.

CLIFTON CLUB (LOST)

The first Clifton Club, a notorious drinking den much frequented by ladies of loose virtue, was at 6 Glebe Street (according to the original numbering system) and it remained in business for 20 years or so between around 1865 and 1885. The premises were demolished and re-built as the Britannia Buildings in 1901. In 1885, meanwhile, the club moved to James Street, now Coronation Terrace, the manager at that time being John Kingdom.

CLIVE CLUB (LOST)

Advertised as a gentleman's drinking club and refreshment rooms, the Clive Club was built when the Penarth Extension Railway line built the original single platform that used to comprise Penarth's town station. By 1878 the club occupied the site of what is today the Railway Hotel. The club's owner/ manager was a Mr J. Jefferies. The club was eventually demolished to make way for the building of what is now the Railway Hotel public house.

CLIVE CONSERVATIVE CLUB (LOST)

The first recorded Conservative Club in the town was the Clive which operated from 54 Windsor Road. It was apparently in operation during the late 1870s and early 1880s under the managership of Mr G M Palmer. The premises were vacated in the mid 1880s when shop fronts were built onto the houses. Number 54 is one of a pair that subsequently became the core of what is today F. W. Woolworth.

CLIVE CRESCENT, COGAN (LOST)

When they were first built in the 1870s, the houses between Bridge Street and Pill Street, Cogan, were in Clive Crescent. Around 1890 the name was changed to Station Terrace, and then a year or two later became Windsor Road. The lane that runs at the rear of the houses is still known as Clive Lane. The name is a reminder of Robert Clive, Baron Plassey, Clive of India. William Pitt in a speech given in the House of Commons when Pitt was Foreign Secretary and Secretary of War in 1757 described him as "a heaven-born general".

COASTGUARD COTTAGES

The town's first Coastguard Cottages overlook the Penarth Marina in Harbour View at the end of Northcliffe Drive. These were established before 1841, and the Census for that year shows that F. A. Weir was the Chief Officer and that there were four boatmen in residence. They lived in the two cottages that are known today as Harbour View. The cottages were built in an advantageous position overlooking the entrance to Cardiff Docks and the Glamorgan Canal Entrance, and gave panoramic views over Penarth Harbour. The coastguard boat was kept in a shed on the shingle promontory that used to run from the foot of the cliff out towards Cardiff. The shingle promontory is now gone, and is instead the site of the entrance to the Marina. A Cardiff Directory for 1855 states: "Letters are brought over [to Penarth] from Cardiff by favour of the crews of the Coastguard Boat.[45]" The Chief Coastguard in 1855 was Lieutenant Quinlan.

The second group of Coastguard Cottages are to be found in Tower Hill which lies between Plymouth Road and Marine Parade. They were opened in 1864. The Coastguard, which was an arm of the Royal Navy during the 19th century, was inspected annually. In 1892 the inspector was Captain Bosanquet and in 1893 Prince Louis Battenberg, father of the late Lord Mountbatten, did the honours[46].

COED-Y-HEBOG (LOST)

This historic place name translates as the Hawk's Wood or Wood of the Hawk. Prior to 19th century urbanization the original wood covered the eastern Cogan escarpment, from the escarpment edge eastwards to cover what is today Wordsworth Avenue, Shakespeare Avenue etc.

[45] Ewen: Directory of Cardiff, 1855.
[46] Penarth Observer, 1892.

The town's first Coastguard Cottage built c.1830's.

COASTGUARD COTTAGES

The town's second Coastguard Cottage built, 1864.

© Diane Mead

Until only recently a pair of kestrels nested each yearin what is left of Coed-y-Hebog, their favourite feeding area being the north face of the Penarth Ridge. Using thermal currents to glide and hover above the overgrown High Local Sidings, one or both of the birds could be seen every day hunting for food. Sadly, recent development work has destroyed this fertile feeding ground and the birds have neither nested nor indeed been seen since 1992.

COGAN

Throughout recorded history there have been many and varied spellings of Cogan, including Cogen (12th century), Kock (1500s); Coggan (1577); Y Cook (1590); Cog (1678); Cogan Vach (1678) and Coggon (1784). The derivation of Cogan is as yet unknown, although two of the more popular theories are that the name could come from the Danish word kog meaning a piece of marshland. This would apply to the glacial basin of modern Cogan, and also to the large depression, a marshy hollow in fact, in the plateau at Old Cogan. Kog also translates as ditched lands, and in the Minister Accounts for 1433-4 we find a reference to "..... wages paid by the Reeve to John Robyns for cleaning and scouring six perches of ditch on Costeneston [Cosmeston] moor at $1\frac{1}{2}$d per perch, paid 9d." This could well have been a reference to the moorland between what is today Old Cogan Hall and the Cosmeston Lakes.

An alternative theory is that Cogan is an artificial form of the Welsh word 'cawe' meaning a dish or bowl or basin. Again this would apply to both the old and more recent Cogan.

In the 12th century, Miles de Cogan accompanied Fitz Stephen to Ireland and saw a great deal of action. In return he was granted the Kingdom of Cork in 1177. He died in 1182.

COGAN CLUB (LOST)

Cogan's first licensed drinking club, as opposed to the numerous shebeens and unlicensed clubs that abounded in the 19th century in this area, was the grandly named Cogan Company Club Limited. It was run from 42 Harriet Street which stands at the junction with Pill Street. The club was managed in the 1870s and 80s by Mr F. Smith. When it closed it became a Mission Hall, being run by Mr Albert Biffert. It later became a shop and has recently been converted into a family home.

25 Harriet Street was in fact one of Cogan's more notorious shebeens. On 24 June 1892 the police raided the house and arrested eight men, three women and a boy, and found beer on tap in both the front and back room[47].

COGAN MOOR (LOST)

Paterson[48] notes the existence of a Cogansmoor in the 13th century. Later references were Cogan Moore, subsequently Cogan Moor. The names relate to an area of low lying land opposite the entrance to Cogan Pill (now approximately the site of Tesco's car park). The land was also known during this same period as the Ely Wharf. The Ely Tidal Harbour was built on the area in the 1850s. This could only be achieved, however, after extensive tipping had raised the level of the land that before this operation had used to flood at high water, especially at the Spring Tides.

In the 13th century, Maurice Ysaac of Llandoch [Llandough] confirmed to the monks of Margam Abbey that he owned an area of marsh land called Coganesmoor - "of which one head stretches from the east upon la slyme which is called Brodeslyme, the other head stretches to the pool called Sammeliswere in length between the Marsh called Pennarismore on the north and the pool called Niwere on the south."

COGAN PILL

The name Cogan Pill is still used to refer to a number of areas and physical features in and around modern Cogan. The pill, a tidal creek, ran inland from the River Ely, marked today by a culvert on the exact location of the pill, just below Tesco's car park. It joined a fast-flowing stream that drained from the Penarth Plateau and Ridge and which used to cut through the Dingle running alongside Windsor Road. The pill and the stream came together at roughly the point where today Little Dock Street stands.

The Dingle stream has been culverted, although it was still shown as a vigorous stream as late as the 1878 Ordinance Survey map of the town.

The land surrounding the pill is also known as Cogan Pill. The Elizabethan mansion that today houses one of the Beefeater chain of restaurants was built in 1554 by Matthew Herbert on a shoulder of ground above the tidal creek. Its

[47] Penarth Observer, 1892.
[48] Paterson: "Early Cardiff", ibid.

official name is Cogan Pill House. (Matthew Herbert, by the way, was a descendent of William Herbert, Earl of Pembroke, who died in 1469. Pembroke Terrace commemorates this connection).

Up until the building of Penarth Dock between 1859 and 1865, the term Cogan Pill was used to describe an area that took in the north and south banks of the River Ely in the vicinity of the mouth of the pill. The embankment built to carry the railway lines to the Dock workings partially blocked the Pill during the late 1850s. In 1884, when work began on lengthening the Dock, the pill was blocked and culverted.

John Bird wrote to the Marquis of Bute on 14 September 1790 that "... the fishermen who have your slime [i.e. mud flats] catch little or no fish ... although a salmon of 30 lbs was, today, caught at Cogan Pill.[49]"

In 1487 Cogan Pill was held by Sir James Tyrell, Sheriff of Glamorgan. By 1610 the manor of Cogan was in the hands of Sir William Herbert and leased to Sir Edward Lewis at a rent of eight pounds, two shillings and a pound of pepper. Also included was a dairy at Cornerswell, the land and stock of which were valued at £32. The stock represented 32 milking cows.

COGAN PILL TILE AND BRICK WORKS (LOST)

Opened in the 1860s, this brickworks continued in operation up until the 1890s when the Penarth Brickworks was opened in Windsor Road, Cogan. The works and its many ovens, buildings, etc. occupied a site where the Leisure Centre stands today.

Amongst other products, the works turned out large and distinctive, almost Mediterranean looking tiles, some of which have withstood the ravages of both time and the developers. Many can still be seen, especially tucked away in the lanes and backwaters of the town, on old stables and blacksmiths' premises.

Early managers of the works included John Hosbans and Henry Millward.

COGAN POST OFFICE

The first Post Office in Cogan was opened in the late 1860s at 2 Hewell Street, the proprietor being William Hughes. The houses were renumbered during the

---

[49]   John Bird's Diaries 1790-1807, edited by Hilary M. Thomas. 1987. Cardiff Library.

1880s and the Post Office became number 50. At this time it was owned by Alfred R. Judd. The house is significantly larger than the other houses in the street and has an arched entrance to one side leading to a coach house and stable. The original wide front window can still be seen, as can the original fittings for the large sun awning.

A later Post Office was opened at 39 Station Terrace, now Windsor Road, in the late 1880s by a Miss E. B. Leaver, and it was still operating in 1895. It stood at the junction of Bridge Street and Windsor Road.

COGAN ROW (LOST) : see Back Row

The name Cogan Row was used up until the early 20th century as an alternative to Back Row.

COGAN TERRACE (LOST)

When the first houses in what is today Grove Place were built in the early 1890s, they were known as Cogan Terrace. They were renamed Grove Place in about 1897. The houses, together with Bute Cottage, were built on land that was a salient of the Cogan Parish and owned by the Bute family. Among the first occupants in 1892 were William Diamond at number 1, James Gould at number 2 and Lewis Parsons at number 3.

COMPANY ROW (LOST)

When the Cogan Pill was dammed it meant houses could be built nearer the Dock rather than behind Back Row, also known as Cogan Row. Between roughly 1861 and the early 1880s the Dock Company put up houses in what is today Pill Street, originally called Company Row.

The Row was built on land raised by the tipping of spoil from the Dock excavations. They housed the men working on the Dock, who came mainly from the West Country and from Ireland. George Lovell and his family came from Yatton, for instance, and William Trenchard also came from Somerset, while numerous Irish families such as the Callaghans, Driscolls, McCarthys, and Sullivans to name but a few worked as coal trimmers and tippers, blacksmiths, shipwrights, riggers and railway workers.

CORBETT ROAD

The name of this road commemorates the Corbett family. In 1854 John Stuart Corbett, a cousin of and agent to the Marquis of Bute, restored and occupied Cogan Pill House. He became a JP and was a powerful force in 19th century Penarth, representing the Bute/Windsor High Church - High Tory control of the town.

CORONATION TERRACE

This terrace was originally built as Church Lane in the 1850s and 60s, before newer houses were built in the 1870s, whereupon it became James Street. It was renamed Coronation Terrace in 1937 to mark the Coronation of George VI. The name James probably commemorated James Andrew Corbett, second son of John Stuart Corbett (see above). James was born in 1846 and died in 1890.

CORNERSWELL COTTAGES (LOST)

These two lovely cottages stood at the Redlands Road end of what is today Hastings Avenue. They were demolished a couple of decades ago to make way for modern houses on the site. The cottages housed workers on Cornerswell Farm. The 1881 Census shows number 1 as being occupied by William Gould, a farm servant, his wife and nine children, together with their servant. Number 2 was occupied by W. Toogood, a farm labourer, his wife and their four children, plus two lodgers. One of Toogood's sons, Sam, became a local bootmaker. He also handled all of the leatherwork at Anderson's Boatyard.

CORNERSWELL FARM (LOST)

The earliest record of a farm sited on what is today's Hastings Close was in 1655, although it is believed a farm had existed even before that. The farm was in the Cogan Parish and its northernmost land was covered by Coed-y-Hebog.

Around 1770 the Marquis of Bute, who owned the parish of Cogan, had the farm rebuilt. It survived right up until 1969 when it was finally demolished. The 1841 Census shows that the farm was occupied by W Roberts, his wife, two visitors, three farm labourers and one house servant.

G O Pierce[50] dates the first recorded reference to a farm as early as 1529, when it was known as Cornelleswell. The derivation comes from the name Cornell(e) and is possibly a connection with the 12th and 13th Century family de Cornely. Alun Morgan[51], meanwhile, suggests the name could refer to St Cornelius, one of the many early Celtic Saints who travelled extensively between Brittany, Cornwall, Ireland and Wales. St Cornelius was a noted wanderer, and could have taken water at the well which stood between the farm and what is today the junction of Redlands Road and Hastings Avenue, perhaps whilst walking from the Monastic settlement at Llandough. There is a Cornelly and a Cornelly Down to the west of Penarth in the Parish of Pyle, as well as a St Cornelly in Brittany.

The land was being farmed in 1855 by a Mr John John.

CORNERSWELL TERRACE (LOST)

In the late 19th and early 20th centuries, before Redlands Road was built, there was a short row of six houses on Redlands Heights. This was known as Cornerswell Terrace. They now form part of the row between St Cyres Road and Redlands Avenue.

COSMESTON

This Norman manor covered an area bounded by today's built up areas of Lower Penarth, Lavernock and Swanbridge. G. O. Pierce[52] suggests the name derives from Robert de Constantin who held the manor from the Earl of Glamorgan in 1166. A few years earlier in 1151 Gilbert de Constantin had given land in Penarth to the Priory of Bristol.

The first recorded name for the manor is Constantineston which appears in 1262. It derives from the Old English 'tun' meaning a village and/or an estate; there have been numerous spellings since, including Costenton (1266), Comestone (1320), Costesmeston (1545), Constantine (1657), and Comaston 1826. Two farms, Lower Cosmeston and Upper Cosmeston, were to be found in the manor until very recently, when Upper Cosmeston was demolished and houses built on the site.

---

[50] G. O. Pierce, ibid.
[51] A. Morgan: Porthcawl Legends.
[52] G. O. Pierce, ibid.

52

COSMESTON CASTLE (LOST)

C. Evans[53] notes "... a little above Lavernock Station [now lost] are the scanty remains of Cosmeston Castle, the messuage of a manor held by a Norman family, de Constantine'. The exact site of the castle is uncertain, but would appear to have been in or near today's reconstructed medieval village.

COUNCIL OFFICES

Built in 1881 on the site of Belle Vue Cottage, this fine imposing building is now empty and in a poor state of repair. It was first the offices of the Penarth Local Board which was set up in 1875. The first meeting of the Boardhad been held at the Penarth Police Station, where Mr Robert Forrest had taken the chair. Consequent meetings were held at 3 Windsor Terrace and continued to be held there until the Albert Road Offices were built. The Penarth Urban District Council, which was set up in the 1890s, later moved to West House in 1945, although some of the clerical staff stayed on at the Belle Vue site until the 1970s.

In the last decade of the 19th century the town had many cases of the killer disease diphtheria, and the Council Offices were converted into a temporary Isolation Hospital for sufferers. The first Matron was a Miss A M Keep and she was followed by a Miss E Harris.

COWSLIP

This name applies to a pathway linking Cogan with Redland Heights. It is now also the name of a housing estate built on fields that slope steeply down from Redlands Road to Cogan.

The derivation remains a mystery, but it could well be that the fields were once covered by cowslips, a beautiful species of the primrose family once commonly found on meadow land. Cowslips, like so many of our native wild flowers, have almost been lost as a result of urban sprawl and modern farming methods.

G O Pierce records the existence of a cowmede (1492) and a cowmead (1783) in the Parish of Cogan[54]. The site or sites of these are unknown, and any connection with Cowslip would appear tenuous.

---

[53] C. Evans: Glamorgan's History and Topography. Revised edition, 1943.
[54] G. O. Pierce, ibid.

CRAVEN WAY

Named after Craven Arms in Shropshire and part of the Windsor/Clive land holdings in that county.

CUSTOM HOUSE

This large imposing building with its distinctive and highly ornate central clock tower was opened in 1865, the same year as the Dock was opened. Hilling[55] describes the building as "pompous, baroquely classical of rusticated stone with projecting wings, corinthian pillars and pedimented gables". It provided office accommodation for a number of officials - Customs and Immigration personnel, the Docks Collector, the Weighing Inspectorate, etc.

The site had previously housed the notorious Penarth Head Inn, built by Penarth's most famous smuggler Edward Edwards.

The building is currently in desperate need of renovation before its fate is sealed and demolition takes place.

CUTT, CWRT

G. O. Pierce[56] makes reference to both the Gutt (c.1700) and the Cutt (1808) and suggests both names refer to the Dingle that runs through Alexandra Gardens alongside Beach Road. He believes the name is a derivation from the Middle English 'cut' or 'cutte', meaning a cut or a water-channel, a natural narrow opening or passage made by water. T. Waring's 1868 map of Penarth shows the Dingle as a fast flowing stream. The 1879 Ordnance Survey also shows a stream passing through the Dingle that runs down from the Glendale Hotel, but this is referred to as the 'cwrt'.

CWM CYDFIN

The Nant Cydfin is a brook that runs through a dense wood and forms a pill where it joins the River Ely. The woody dell and the pill are known as Cwm Cydfin, and the pill forms the boundary between the parishes of Llandough and Leckwith. The name Cydfin is probably a corruption of a Welsh personal name.

---

[55]   Hilling: Glamorgan Historian, volume 7.
[56]   G O Pierce, ibid.

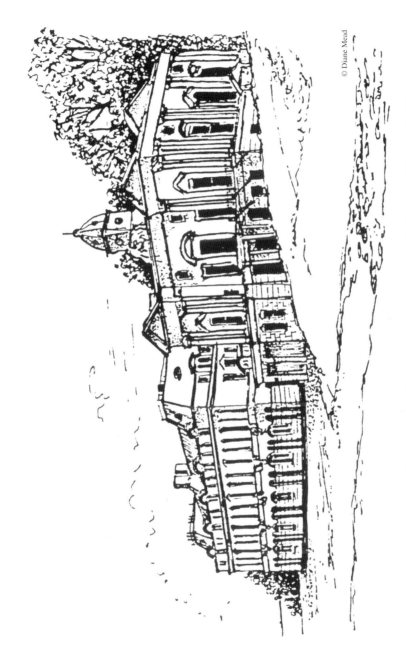

The Custom House, with tower, and the Dock Buildings also known as the Marine Buildings built 1864.

The pill shows us how Cwtsh-y-Cwm and the other pills in the Penarth parish would have looked. It is best seen at either high water or at low water and the best vantage point is the new Ely Link Road.

CWRT-YR-ALA

This grand mansion standing in a beautiful leafy setting is known by the local Welsh name. Its derivation is from Court y Rayley, which dates back to 1657.

Simon de Raleigh, an ancestor of Sir Walter Raleigh, married Joanna de Reigny in the 13th century. She inherited the manors of Wrinstone, Michaelston-le-pit, and Llantwit. The house was at various times known as Cwrt Raleagh (14th century), Court y Rayle (1695), Cwrt y Ralla (1844) and several others beside[57].

CWRT-Y-VIL CASTLE

Old Ordnance Survey maps show a reference to a " 'Castle (ruined)' in an area near the entrance to what is today Castle Avenue, although there is no evidence to support this claim. The area was also reported to be the site of a chantry (see Chantry Rise).

Cwrt can be translated as a court or mansion (large house). Certainly a farm had stood on the site in 1700. It was at that time called Courtyvill. The farm's main building may well have been castellated, hence the origin of the castle myth. And we also know there was a building on the site even prior to Courtyvill Farm in 1700. Bevan[58] suggests that the ruins known as Cwrt-y-Vil Castle were in fact the remains of 'an old ecclesiastical manor house'.

Vil could be a corruption of le Veel (Vele), the name of a family that had held St. Fagans and the surrounding lands in the 13th and 14th centuries. In 1274 Robert le Veel, a bailiff visiting the area on behalf of the Earl of Gloucester, was arrested for seizing a ship and its cargo in the port of Barry on Tuesday, 10 April 1274, the property of Henry of Caen[59]. He was tried at the King's Assize and imprisoned in Cardiff Castle. There was no definite le Veel connection with Penarth, although subsequent owners of St. Fagans, notably

---

[57] Barry: The Centenary Book. Edited by Donald Moore. 1984.
[58] E.T. Bevan, ibid.
[59] Barry: The Centenary Book. Edited by Donald Moore. 1984.

Sir Edward Lewis of the Van, Caerphilly, did hold large tracts of land in and around Penarth. So too did Other Windsor, the Third Earl of Plymouth, as a result of his marriage to Elizabeth Lewis of the Van in the early 18th century.

By 1700 Courtyvil Farm was being worked by John Perkins. A few years later in 1720, the farm was being run by Florence Waters and comprised 109 acres. The 1841 Census shows R. John, his wife and three children as living at the farm, together with two servants. By 1881 the occupants were Hezekiah Greatrex, his wife, daughter and son.

CWRT-Y-VIL HOUSE (LOST)

A magnificent grand mansion built in the 1870s, Cwrt-y-Vil House at that time stood in splendid isolation on what today forms the junction of Lavernock Road and Victoria Road. The house was surrounded by extensive landscaped gardens, and had a curved avenue of trees linking the house with the charming lodge at the main gates. The site of the demolished house is now Stanwell School's all-weather sports area, and all that remains is a section of the stone boundary wall and five or six mature trees that had been planted to form the original avenue. Even these are now under threat.

The house was built for Lascelles Carr, an impulsive and eccentric Yorkshireman, who was the owner and editor of the Western Mail, which he bought from the Marquis of Bute in 1877. Lloyd George described Carr as "the cleverest man I have ever met". And Cecil Rhodes said of him, "Give me Lascelles Carr in South Africa, and I will take the world!".

During July 1892 Carr borrowed the town steamroller for a few days from the Local Board on the "usual terms" to roll the new carriage drive to Cwrt-y-Vil House. For part of 1892 Lascelles Carr moved to Tredelerch House, Rhymney, Cardiff, but soon moved back to Cwrt-y-Vil House.

The Penarth Wesleyans held their 1892 Whitsun Outing at Cwrt-y-Vil. It was reported that "Mr W. B. Gibbs kindly threw open his extensive and well-stocked grounds and allowed them use of his field". This now forms part of the Stanwell School playing field.

Whilst on the subject of the Wesleyans, who played a major role in Penarth's advancement, in July 1892 the death was announced of the Rev. James William Hay Carr of Kingston-on-Hull. He was the son of the late Rev. James Carr, who for many years had been the highly respected Wesleyan minister at Dinas

Powis, and ironically the father of Lascelles Carr, a man who was generally disliked.

From around 1900 the house was the home of the Pyman family, one of the town's major ship owning families. During the Second World War the American Allied forces established an extensive holding camp in the grounds and set up serried ranks of Quonset huts. With the cessation of hostilities, the camp was taken over by the GPO's Engineering Regional Training School and used as an accommodation and training camp, the original house by this time having been demolished.

At some time around the turn of the century, the name of the house was changed to Raithwaite.

CWTSH-Y-CWM (LOST)

This is the name given to the pill that bisected the extensive, curved, shingle beach that ran from Anderson's Boatyard around under the Penarth Head, then up the south side of the River Ely to a spot about halfway along the old Dock. The pill entered the river approximately at the point where the Junction Locks form the link between the DockBasin and the main Dock. The remains of the Junction Locks can still be seen.

The beach and the pill were lost with the building of the Dock. Prior to this, the pill had been used by early (i.e. pre-1859) residents of Penarth, by the Coastguard, Channel pilots and fisherman, who all moored their craft in the pill. The extensive and sheltered shingle beach had also been taken advantage of by all the early visitors to Penarth, including the Beaker Folk, the Romans, Irish and Viking sea-raiders, early Celtic Saints, the Norman lord Robert Fizhamon and various smugglers and pirates.

Using Flat Holm as their base, the smugglers Richard and Pasco Robinson, who were father and son, used to run goods from Guernsey to the island and used small boats manned by local runners to land their contraband at the pill. Pirates such as Simon Fferdinando, John Callice, William Chick and Tom Clark all landed their prizes at Cwtsh-y-Cym. Clark was arrested at Penarth in 1578, charged with terrorizing the local inhabitants and 'forcing them to victual his vessel'. In 1584, Sir John Chichester wrote to Sir Edward Stradling about a vessel of his that had been taken on passage to Biscay from Ilfracombe - "[T]he pirate Storey was reported to be at the Ellye ooze near Cardiff[60]". And

---

[60]   E. L. Chappell: History of the Port of Cardiff. 1939.

in January 1586 another marauder by the name of Beere was described as "... a pyratt ridinge with a prize in the harborough at Pennarthe".

The pill was fed from the land by a number of streams that drained down from the Head and the Ridge. The main such stream ran from the Head through the front of what is now Headlands School then through the grounds of the Northcliff and Mariner's Heights housing estates. Before Mariner's Heights was constructed, a lengthy section of a deep and wide dried-out water course could still be seen in the grounds of Northcliff. Despite having been culverted, this stream still breaks out in the area of land around the former High Level Sidings.

G. O. Pierce[61] suggests that Cwtsch-y-Cwm can mean a whole range of things including a couch, resting place, cover, a little corner, alternatively a hiding place, a kennel or small shed, outhouse, cot or similar building[62]. E. A. Benjamin also suggests dog kennel, but he places Cwtsh-y-Cym as a cottage close to the Kymin. In fact the cottage that bore the same name as the pill was a substantial building, possibly one of a pair that used to stand on the east bank of the pill. This particular housewas also known as the Pilot's Cottage.

The 1841 Census shows that the occupants were Elias England and his wife. By 1855, just before it was demolished in fact, the occupant was D. Morgan.

The pill, the streams, the shingle beach and the cottage were all lost when work started on the Dock excavations in 1859.

On 10 September 1791, Judge Hardinge, who had been appointed Solicitor General in 1782 and who went on to become Attorney General to Queen Anne in 1794, took a boat from the Cwtsh-y-Cym pill to sail to Minehead. He was accompanied by a Mr Hollier, who lived at Adamsdown House in Cardiff, on the site now occupied by Cardiff Prison. Hollier was Chief Steward to the Marquis of Bute, as well as an Alderman, Bailiff, Town Clerk and Collector of Port Customs. Hardinge was to be immortalised as the 'Waggish Welsh Judge' in Byron's Don Juan.

DAGGERTOWN

Daggertown is a colloquial name for a sub-division of the Bowery. When I was younger I thought it was just a romantic appellation, useful for bestowing some

---

[61] G. O. Pierce. Ibid.
[62] E. A. Benjamin, Penarth 1841-1871. (1980).

colour and character on an otherwise rather drab area, an attempt to acquire a degree of social cachet. Research, however, shows the name to be particularly apt.

The geographical area covered by Daggertown is hard to pinpoint, but a convenient definition might be the area stretching from the Royal Hotel up as far as the Golden Lion, then down Queen's Road (formerly Maughan Street) and on to the old Penarth Hotel, now Headlands School. It would also have to include the short streets and lanes leading off and parallel to Queens Road and the Dock area itself.

In the 19th century this small area was rumoured to have contained as many as nine public houses, five legal drinking clubs, to say nothing of the numerous shebeens, brothels and seamen's boarding houses that had been set up, usually by mainland Europeans - Germans, Dutchmen and so on.

The area was cosmopolitan, vibrant, vigorous and violent, with almost daily assaults, murders, robberies and stabbings. The police regularly had to draw their cutlasses. The following four examples show just what a violent and dangerous place Daggertown was up to the end of the last century.

On 19 September 1892, a case was brought before two Justices of the Peace, Major Thornley and J. P. Thompson, sitting in session at Penarth. The court heard the case against Jeremiah Lynch, a boarding house keeper of Maughan Terrace who was accused of having stabbed Julius Franz, a Russian seaman, in the head. Evidence was given that "Franz staggered into the next room and Mary Sims of Dock Road stated that 'Franz came into the kitchen bleeding from the forehead and from behind the ear.' The case was adjourned for a week.

On 8 January 1892 the Penarth Observer reported another harrowing tale. On Tuesday, 5 January, Sam Buckland, 77, and his wife, who was 76, were taken from 30 John Street and interred together at St. Augustine's Churchyard. Fifteen years previously there had been another double funeral from this same house. In 1877, Charles Tree, a rigger at the Docks who had previously worked as a sail-maker, had returned from work and 'beat out his wife's brains with a large rigger's fid and then cut his own throat.'

On 22 January 1892 O'Connell Price, a steward on the barque Gazelle, which was lying at Penarth Dock, used a knife to stab John Houghton, a seaman on board the same vessel.

Joseph Organ, a hawker, was charged on 10 February 1891 with brutally assaulting his wife in Maughan Street. He was said to have been very drunk

and beating his wife cruelly. During the course of the fight both fell out of their
van.

DARDANELLES

This name, which is very familiar to old Penarthians, is used to describe an
area of the beach and cliff, roughly between the multi-storey car park and the
Penarth Head. It is generally accepted that servicemen returning from the
Great War gave it this nickname - many, of course, having served in the
Dardanelles campaign. In fact a large number of Penarth men went to
Gallipoli, many of them dock workers and tugboat men, where they served on
the hundreds of tugs and barges used to get men and munitions ashore in the
shallow waters of the real Dardanelles.

During the Second World War the American Forces established an anti-
aircraft emplacement protected with sand bags on the plateau covering the
sewer outfall chamber at the Dardanelles. There is no record of those guns ever
having been fired in anger.

DAVIES' DAY SCHOOL

This was one of the many small private schools that proliferated in Penarth
during the nineteenth century. The school operated from 30 Westbourne Road
during the closing decades of the last century, when a Miss Davies was both
its Proprietor and Principal.

DINGLE(s)

Dingle is a word usually said to describe a wooded dell, and there are
numerous examples in and around Penarth. The best known, perhaps, is the
Windsor Road Dingle, which is a deep and wide water course cut by a vigorous
stream that used to be fed by smaller streams draining from the Penarth Ridge
and the Penarth Plateau.

Before the 1878 Penarth Extension Railway was opened with its single track
running from the Docks at Cogan to Penarth, the main stream ran from the area
of what is todayVictoria Square, down through a woody dell or grove, now
Grove Terrace. It then dog-legged at the point where Grove Terrace meets West
Terrace and flowed for a while towards the Dingle before running down to the
pill at Cogan. The building of the railway embankment and later urbanization

entailed the construction of a sewerage and drainage system, at which time the stream was contained in a large culvert. Parts of the Dingle were utilized in the 1880s as the town's first official refuse dump.

The Local Board received many complaints from the residents of the newly built houses in Lower Plassey Street complaining about the smell. (The original Plassey Street and Lower Plassey Street, incidentally, were renamed simply Plassey Street when renumbering took place in 1890.)

Other dingles include the two that run through Alexandra Park, Beach Road and the Glendale dingle. Both were originally very fast-flowing streams. Another is now known as the Kymin, while a shorter dingle runs down to the foreshore at the southern end of Penarth Yacht Club.

DOCK BEACH

The Dock Beach is an expanse of shingle and pebbles which is now under threat from the plans of the Cardiff Bay Development Corporation. It stretches from the Black Bench and round the massive pitching that protects the Custom House and Dock Buildings from the high tides. The beach was always well patronized for bathing and picnicking purposes by the Bowery kids, who preferred it to the Donkey Beach. It was also extensively used by American servicemen during the Second World War, especially at night, for what can loosely be classified as Rest and Recreation!

DOCK BEACH HILL

The road that ran from the Royal Hotel down to the Dock entrance was originally known as Dock Road. Following urbanization, the built-up areas became Paget Road and Paget Terrace. The steep slope to the Dock became Dock Entrance Road, although it was then and still is known to Bowery kids as Dock Beach Hill.

The 'hill' was in fact cut into the north face of Penarth Ridge when the Dock was opened in 1865. Prior to this the path down to the River Ely and Cwtsh-y-Cym ran westward (towards Cogan), down the northern edge of the Penarth Road.

DOCK BUILDINGS

This large, imposing and attractive block built in the French style stands alongside the Custom House at the bottom of Dock Beach Hill. Both buildings were opened in 1865. The upper floors of the building used to be used as accommodation while there were a range of shops on the ground floor. At the seaward end could be found the Marine Hotel and at the Custom House end a Post and Telegraphic Office, which was regularly used by ships' captains, agents and owners. In between could be found the premises of T J Williams (Optician), W. D. John (Chemist), W. Gay (Green Grocer), T. B. Clode (Ships' Butcher), Davies & Son (Ships' Chandlers) and Luen and Hall (Marine Store Dealers).

Hilling[63] '... alongside the Custom House is a bold French renaissance style three storey terrace, for Penarth a rare example of Victorian housing on a grand scale ..... the elegant main floor [ground floor] is divided into five units of three bays.'

Harry Martin remembers the time when little coasting ketches used to load up with coal from Ely Harbour destined for the West Country or Ireland. If they were threatened by southerly gales they would often ride out the bad weather anchored on the safe mud of the Penarth Flats and "... that's when the little Post Office done a bit of trade"[64].

Both the Custom House and the Dock Buildings are in a poor state of repair following a serious fire, and could well be lost to the town.

DOCK COTTAGES (LOST)

When Penarth Dock was opened in 1865 there were two official entrances by road, the Dock Entrance Road (Dock Beach Hill) and the Penarth Dock Road, which ran from what is today's Auto Valet Service across the new Tesco car park. There were three cottages on the Penarth Dock Road during the 1860s, 70s and 80s. Number one was occupied by Archie Boland, a dock bargeman, his wife and seven children. Number two was occupied by G. Walters and his family, while Mr and Mrs Brookes lived at number 3 and used part of their cottage to operate a tea room.

When the Dock was lengthened in the 1880s the cottages were demolished and extensive locomotive sheds were built on the site. When the Penarth Extension Railway was constructed in 1878 the road disappeared and a small subway was built to replace the road and maintain a right of way. The subway

[63] Hilling, ibid notes.
[64] Penarth Past Oral History Society: "We Remember It Well", ibid.

can still be seen directly behind the Auto Valet Service Station in Windsor Road.

DOCK ENTRANCE ROAD
See Dock Beach Hill.

DOCK HOTEL
One of the town's original public houses, the Dock Hotel was built in the 1850s. Its official name was the Penarth Dock Hotel, although it was always known simply as the Dock Hotel. When it was built, the pub was in the wildest part of Daggertown - Maughan Place - which in the 1860s became Maughan Terrace. The pub was a notorious haven and watering place for seamen and members of the many nefarious sub-cultures of Daggertown - prostitutes and their pimps, crimps, etc.

The 1861 Census shows the landlord as one Mr W. Price who was born in Merthyr, his wife and four daughters and one son, together with four paying guests - an engineer, two carpenters and one foreman, all no doubt employed on the building of the Dock.

The fortunes of the pub declined as the Docks trade fell off. On 6 July 1936 the dock closed to commercial shipping, although the pontoon was kept open for ship repairs and the Ely Tidal Harbour remained open for business. The pub, however, was closed. The Dock itself was re-opened in July 1940 after the country went to war.

The pub itself became a rooming house, and was eventually converted into flats.

In the 1860s and right up until his business was bought by Soloman Andrews, David Lewis Williams, the landlord of the Dock Hotel, ran horse buses from the pub into St. Marys Street, Cardiff. In 1871 Andrews brought three horse buses, seven horses, and all their harnesses from Mr Williams.

A particularly colourful neighbour of Williams's in Maughan Terrace in the early 1870s was a Mrs Sarah Heap, who was described as a 'steamboat owner'.

DOCK ROAD
When the original Town Plan was drawn up the road from the Royal Hotel leading at that time down to the Dock entrance was given the startlingly

original name of Dock Road. By the time the houses were built in the 1870s and 80s, Dock Road was divided into sections known as Paget Road, Paget Terrace and Dock Entrance Road. Older Penarthians still refer to it by its old name, Dock Road.

DOCK SUBWAY

This architectural gem, a monument to Victorian engineering, ran from the end of Dock Subway Road, under the wide and extensive High Level Sidings, before emerging on the southern side of the Dock, between coal tips numbers 8 and 9. The subway was the umbilical cord linking the town to its genesis, the Dock, and was the main artery through which poured thousands of dock-workers, crane-drivers, coal tippers and trimmers, riggers and shipwrights and shell-backed mariners from every corner of the world.

At the Billy Banks end of the Dock Subway Road, entry was gained via a flight of wide steep steps capped with heavy blocks of Radyr redstone. The subway itself was about seventy yards long and beautifully constructed out of local yellow brick, local white tiles and Radyr redstone, with Staffordshire blue bricks used for capping and edging. The subway is still in existence, but can no longer be used by the public since both entrances have been blocked off and the area covered over.

The subway was originally constructed to allow easy and safe access to the Dock. It meant workers no longer had to risk their lives crossing the busy and dangerous sidings. They could avoid the continuous "Fly-shunting" operations and the sunken railway lines laid in cuttings, some as deep as 12 feet. Unfortunately many men ignored the safe route and paid the price. In October 1892, Lauritz Matthausen and other crewmen from the Swedish ship, S.S. Bris went into the centre of the town to shop. This turned into a heavy drinking session, and eventually they left their last watering hole, the Royal Hotel, and staggered down Dock Subway Road. They all entered the subway save for Matthausen, who started to cross the sidings where he fell into one of the sunken sidings. Despite being seriously injured, he managed to climb out and safely negotiated the rest of the sidings, only to fall down the steep cliff face onto the dock side below, badly smashing his head. He was found at about 6 a.m by a dock worker, Mr Langham, and taken on board the S.S. Bris, where Dr. Nell was called, but theSwedish sailor had died from his injuries.

DOCK SUBWAY ROAD (LOST)

This road ran from opposite the Royal Hotel, down a steep incline, skirted the lime kilns, then continued as far as the Subway stairs. The road was lost during the building of Prince Charles Court.

DOLLY STEPS

This charming flight of steps runs down from the Glendale Hotel on Plymouth Road, following the Dingle path alongside the Cutt and it used to be one of the more attractive walkways linking the town with the sea front. These days it is overgrown and the victim of fly-tipping although some remedial work is now being undertaken.

The origin of the name Dolly Steps is not known, although the diminutive may offer a clue. The steps were built at the turn of the 20th century, in around 1905 in fact, to replace a sloping path which had been unsafe in wet weather. For generations, parents taking small children down the steps used them to teach the youngsters to count.

DONKEY BEACH

This name is still used to describe the stretch of Penarth foreshore between the Yacht Club slipway and the Dardanelles, and to differentiate it from Dock Beach. Many were the bloody arguments among Bowery Boys of my generation as to the virtues or otherwise of the Donkey Beach compared with Dock Beach. Both had their partisan supporters.

The name reminds us that for generations donkeys were worked along the narrow strip of shingle between the Pier and the Yacht Club when the tide was out, and along the Promenade when the tide was in. The donkeys were stabled in various places in the Bowery, and two sites can still be seen - one in Ludlow Street (behind the O.A.P.'s meeting place at Arcot Street Hall), the other at 35 King Street, where the original stable and yard are still in excellent order.

Sadly the donkeys were badly used and ill-treated. At the Penarth Magistrates Court on 29 July 1892, Harry Jones, aged 13, a donkey boy, was charged with cruelty to the donkeys on the beach. Inspector Lockwood had seen the boy beating the animals unmercifully. Sadly this was an all too common occurrence, and a cause of continual complaint by the public to both the local press and the police. Jones, by the way, was fined half a crown.

DONKEY ISLAND

The name Donkey Island has two possible derivations. In early times, goods, both legal and illegal, were transported to and from Penarth by donkeys. In the late 19th and early 20th centuries, donkeys plied their trade on the Penarth foreshore. (See Donkey Beach).

The reference to an 'island' is self-explanatory if you can imagine an aerial view of Penarth before 1850. At high water in particular, Penarth would be virtually surrounded by the sea. Imagine the stretch from Lavernock Point to the Head, but also south-westwardly to the Bendrick Rock with the flooded estuary between Barry and Sully pushing water up almost as far as Dinas Powis. The river Ely stretched along the northern boundary from the Head to Cogan Pill, and if we add the flooded Cogan Basin, it is easy to visualise how it might be described as an 'island'.

DRILL HALL

During the 19th century, Penarth housed numerous military detachments, including the Rifle Corps, a Cycle Brigade, various Artillery groups, plus a detachment of the Severn Sub-marine Miners. The town's first Drill Hall was opened in the 1860s at 9 Maughan Street (see Artillery Barracks). Later a Drill Hall stood on the site of what is today Monty Smith's Garage on the corner of Railway Terrace and Windsor Road. The town's main Drill Hall, however, was built between 1896-7 in Woodland Place. Sadly, it was demolished in 1994 to make way for a housing development. This marked the loss of the town's last military memorial, and dealt yet another blow to the town's history and heritage.

DROS-Y-MOR

This truly magnificent mansion, a grand and palatial building of local yellow brick was built in the 1890s. Its first occupant was John Duncan, later Sir John Duncan, a member of a famous local family who were ship owners and newspaper proprietors. The house stood in extensive landscaped gardens, and had a private chapel attached to the main house at its northern end. It also boasted a large quadrangular-shaped detached block of buildings containing stables and coach houses, with servants' accommodation above. In later years the house was home to the Callaghan family, another of the town's wealthy ship owning elite. S. H. Callaghan took up residence there in 1916.

The house used to overlook the Windsor Gardens and the Bristol Channel. Sadly, it was demolished in 1971 to make way for a housing estate, and all that remains is a long section of the original boundary wall.

DYSERTH ROAD

The Windsor/Clive family owned extensive estates in North Wales, including the picturesque village of Dyserth and its surrounding lands. Lord Windsor owned a large mansion known as Plas-yn-Dyserth. He also held all the mineral rights to the estate in the beautiful Vale of Clwyd.

EDGELL'S (LOST)

During the last decades of the 19th century, Miss Mary Ann Edgell ran a small private school for young ladies known as Edgell's Private Ladies School. The establishment operated from 71 Windsor Road, and was opened in 1884.

EMPIRE PALACE (LOST)

Mr White was the second man to open a cinema in Penarth when he took out a lease on 19 Glebe Street in 1911 and opened the Cinema Palace. He subsequently rechristened it with the more grandiose title Empire Palace in about 1914. The cinema was sold to Mr Shorthouse in 1918, and the building now forms part of the Penarth Social Club.

ECHNI (LOST)

Echni is the earliest recorded name for Flat Holm and is referred to on a number of occasions in the Liber Landavensis. In 620 AD King Tewdric, his sons and their followers fought against the invading Saxons. Having been mortally wounded, the King requested he be buried on Echni, and his final wish was honoured.

ELY OOZE (LOST)

This name for the River Ely, which was first used in Norman times, enjoyed common currency right up until the 19th century. Given that ooze is derived from an Anglo-Saxon word meaning mud or slime, and that Ely is a corruption of the Welsh Elai, which also means mud or slime, the name literally translates as mud mud or slime slime.

In 1584 Sir John Chichester wrote to Sir Edward Stradling, the Queen's Commissioner for Piracy on the Glamorgan Sea Board that "... a barke, freightered by my friends and myself ... departed from Ilfracombe for Biscay ... next day seized by an Englishman named Storie sailing under the flag of Don Anthonio (the natural son of Lewis, Duke of Beja, who was himself a son of Emmanuel the Great, King of Portugal) ... the vessel was of three score and ten tons ... and is lying about the Ellye oose[65]".

As late as 1840, Captain Smythe, Marine Superintendent to Lord Bute, during evidence given to a Parliamentary Commission investigating the proposed building of a dock at Cogan Pill, continually referred to the "Ely ooze[66]".

ELY WHARF (LOST)

The term wharf in this context is derived from Early English and means an embankment, grassy dyke or a raised bank usually on low lying land that is either marshy or near water. It is still used in England. The name has nothing to do with a dockside wharf.

The term Ely Wharf was used right up until the early 19th century and can be found on old maps and documents and in old books. It referred to the land on the north bank of the River Ely directly opposite the Cogan Pill entrance. The land was raised by extensive tipping during the early 1850s when it was used to develop the Ely Tidal Harbour, including the construction of coal staiths, warehouses, sidings and two large wooden dockside wharves. One of these was used to unload mixed goods, and the other to unload iron ore. All can still be seen, although they are in a sadly ruinous state.

ESPLANADE HOTEL

The Esplanade Hotel was a wonderful Victorian pile. Built in 1887, it was an architectural gem constructed out of locally produced bricks and imported Bath stone. By the time it was destroyed by fire on 20 May 1977 it had become

---

[65] E. L. Chappell, ibid.
[66] Smythe, ibid.

Coal staiths at the Ely Tidal Harbour.

70

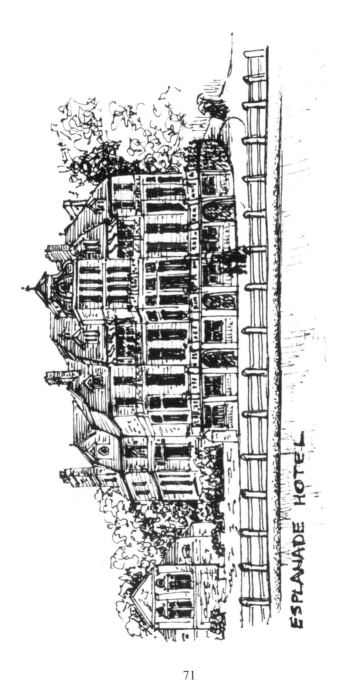

The "swaggering, garish" Esplanade Hotel.

71

a veritable time machine and appeared to contain the original furniture and fittings, and, it was rumoured, staff! Hilling describes the Esplanade as a "..... swaggering, garish red brick building[67]".

Enjoying panoramic views across the Bristol Channel to the Somerset coast, the hotel was hugely popular and became the Penarth home from home of the world-famous Barbarian Rugby Club, who played their first game against Penarth in 1901.

During the 19th century the hotel also housed the Penarth Banjo Club, whose membership included several of the town's young swells and sons of local shipowners and other dignitories, who met there weekly. Their numbers included the Batchelor brothers of Uppercliff, Emile Aicard of Plymouth Road, R. Weichert of 'Hillside', Beach Road, and Mr Culley, whose family owned the Philharmonic in Cardiff, the Exchange Restaurant in Cardiff Docks, and the Chain Locker at Barry Dock. Mr Kerpen, who was the proprietor of the hotel, was also a member. There were usually about 20 banjo players at the weekly meetings, and one zither player.

The Penarth Debating Society also met at the Hotel once a month. At their January 1892 meeting they took as their topic "Wealth" (being no doubt well qualified to discuss this in detail!), before going on to discuss the need for a Free Library in the town "... to give the working class access to books[68]". The town's first library, incidentally, was opened on 5 October1894 in Arcot Street.

EVENLODE AVENUE

The Evenlode is a tributary of the River Thames and runs through the Stanwell Estates of the Windsor family. It was here that Othoere (Other), a Norse Viking, first settled:- "Othoere, the old sea captain who dwelt in Heligoland"[69] is commemorated as the discoverer of the far North Cape. This feat is referred to in the appendix to King Alfred's translation of Orosuis, later put into verse by Longfellow. Othoere lived on the banks of the Evenlode, and it is from him that the Windsor family are descended. His grandson, Walter, took the name de Windsor and was created Baron Windsor during the reign of William the Conqueror.

---

[67] Hilling, ibid.
[68] Penarth Observer, 1892.
[69] W. T. Williams : Windsor Monograph.

72

FERNS

The Ferns was a large and imposing, albeit rather grim, house built for the Penarth Dock Master in 1864 as the Dock was nearing completion. The Census of 1871 shows that Lt. (later Captain) James Poole, R.N.R. was the resident, with his first wife, Olivia, their two daughters, a governess, a cook and a parlour maid. In 1888 the occupant was Captain Walter Henry Pengelley, R.N.

The house, which was set in large enclosed gardens, was built on the northern side of the Penarth Ridge and afforded panoramic views over Cardiff and the Penarth Docks, as well as the upper reaches of the Bristol Channel. The house was recently demolished and others built on the site. All that remains of the original is a section of the massive boundary wall. The house was also, incidentally, known as the 'Dock House'.

FERRIS'S BOYS' SCHOOL (LOST)

At the turn of the century, Miss Ferris was running a Boys' School from 13 Stanwell Road, the building today being part of Westbourne School. From 1897 until 1900 Miss Ferris had also operated an earlier Boys' Preparatory School from Ebenezar House, Westbourne Road, which had in turn been used as the Penarth Grammar School between the early 1880s and 1897.

FERRY LANE

A steep lane, stepped and cobbled, linking Queens Road (Maughan Street) to Paget Terrace (Dock Road), Ferry Lane had no direct connection with the River Ely Ferry other than the fact that as one descended the cobbled steps the Ferry and its landing places could be clearly seen on both sides of the river.

Passengers from the steam ferry that linked Cardiff to Penarth between 1857 and 1903 used to disembark at the Dock, and a steam-driven chain ferry ran between the north and south banks of the River Ely. If the chain was out of service or if it had broken down, rowing boats were used instead[70].

---

[70]   Rowlands, ibid.

FIRE ENGINE STATION

During the 1870s the town's first fire fighting appliance was housed at the Plassey Street end of what is today the Britannia Buildings. Mr John Evans was the manager of the private insurance company that owned the appliance. The cobbled yard can still be seen behind the launderette and taxi office at the junction of Glebe Street and Plassey Street.

During the 1880s the fire engine was housed at the Police Station but moved to the new purpose built Fire Station next door to the Council Offices in Albert Road in about 1908.

Before the first fire engine was introduced in Penarth in 1875 any fire in the town had to be attended by the fire engine from Cardiff. So when a fire broke out on the barque Psyche, which had left London, to load a cargo of steam coal and was berthed in Penarth Dock prior to sailing for Shanghai, the manual engine, with Fireman Williams in charge, had to come out from Cardiff. The appliance left Cardiff at 1.45 p.m. and arrived at the Dock at 2.10 p.m., with more firemen subsequently arriving from Cardiff by cab[71].

FISHERS (LOST)

During the 19th century a large school was established at 6 and 7 Church Street (now Church Road). It was owned and run by Mrs E. H. Fisher, assisted by, among others, her two daughters, the Misses Fisher. The school (its full title was Fisher's Ladies College) was based in two particularly large and attractive Victorian town houses. Between roughly 1875 and 1885 the school had operated from 8 Windsor Road, but moved to Church Street in 1885 where it advertised itself as a Day and Boarding School: "All the comforts of home are secured by boarders, and the greatest care is taken of their health". In addition to Mrs Fisher and her daughters, the teaching staff had a number of both male and female teachers. Mrs Fisher's husband was the Rev William Fisher, Chaplain to the Seamens' Mission. The school can justly claim to be the town's first private school.

FLATHOLM

The holm, which is made up of 43 acres of carboniferous limestone formed some 280,000,000 years ago, lies alongside Steep Holm as a sentinel guarding

---

[71] Cardiff Times, 23 December 1871.

the entrance to the Severn Sea. The island has been used for various activities and there is a long list of occupants. Many of the early Welsh Saints, including Barruc, Cadoc and Gildas, stayed on the island as anchorites, especially during Lent. Barruc, also known as Finbarr, became the Patron Saint of Cork and was drowned whilst sailing from the island towards the South Wales Coast. He is buried on Barry Island.

In 1067 Queen Gytha, mother of King Harold, sought sanctuary with an "entourage of many distinguished men's wives". Several centuries later, when Henry VIII was suppressing the monasteries, the Black Friars of Cardiff fled to and sought sanctuary on Flat Holm.

Irish raiders, Vikings, smugglers and pirates all used the Island. In fact it was the Vikings who gave it the name Flat Holm, which is derived from the Old Norse words holmr (river island) and flatter (flat). The Normans called the island Platam Holmon. Documents from the 12th century show that William, Earl of Gloucester, Lord of Glamorgan, signed a deed bequeathing "Three acres dedicated to Santo Michael's et Santo Cadoc et Dolfino (Dyfan) on the island in the sea at Penarth". A charter dating from the same period granted to the St Augustine's Abbey in Bristol also makes reference to the ownership of Flat Holm: "Platam Holmon with the chapels in that island and the living of the island and the church and lands at Rumney.

In the 1730s, when the island was owned by the Marquis of Bute, it was leased by William Crispe, a Bristol merchant who, with the support of the Merchant Venturers of Bristol, petitioned the Elders of Trinity House to erect a lighthouse on the island. The first light was shown in 1738.

In June 1791 the Lord Mount Stuart sent miners to the island in what proved to be an abortive attempt to re-open the ancient lead workings[72].

FORREST ROAD

Robert Forrest was agent to the Windsor Estate and played a major role in the building and development of Penarth, which was one of the country's first planned towns. It was built to plans prepared by John Wolfe Barry for Lady Windsor, the plans being known officially as the "Penarth Development Plan".

Forrest lived in grand style at a house known as 'Greenwood' in St Fagans and treated Penarth as his personal fief until his power was challenged in the

---

[72] Bird's Diaries, ibid.

late 1880s and early 1890s by the emerging middle-class of religious and political non-conformists. Forrest gave a talk in Penarth on 22 July 1892 following a formal luncheon at the Golf Club, during which he described how: "When I [first] came to Penarth, I saw some tumble-down farms and a few streets that were most difficult to walk along[73]".

GAY STREET (LOST)

Gay Street is mentioned in street directories for the 1890s, although at that time it contained just one house, 'Ardlour', the home of a Mr W H Eidman. During the first week of May 1897 a Mr Hancock presented plans to the Penarth Urban District Council forthree villas to be built in the street. By 1900 Gay Street had become Victoria Avenue. The derivation of Gay is as yet unknown, although a Mr John Gay was a Reader at the Mission to Seamen on the Dock in the 1880s. Also, the name of the town's first lifeboat, launched on 28 January 1861, was the George Gay, named in honour of her donor[74]. It was renamed the Lady Windsor in 1865.

GEM (LOST)

The Empire Palace was taken over for a short period by a Mr Shorthouse who re-named it The Gem. It stayed open for business for roughly thirteen years between 1915 and 1928.

GEORGE (LOST)

Local legend has it that Humphries' Sub-Post Office in Queen's Road was a public house during the 19th century, when it was known as 'The George'. Extensive research, however, has failed to establish the existence of any such pub. It could be that the 'George' was a local name for the drinking club known officially as the Beaufort.

Mr Fanning[75] suggests that a Pat O'Sullivan used to run a public house next door to the Royal Hotel, although he gives no dates, and here again no evidence can be found to substantiate this claim.

---

[73] Penarth Observer, 1892.
[74] Graham Farr : Wreck & Rescue in the Bristol Channel.
[75] Fanning, ibid.

GIBBS HOME

The Taff Vale Railway opened their Penarth Hotel in 1868[76] It was never a commercial success and the staff invariably outnumbered the paying guests.

In 1917 Major John Angel Gibbs, DSO, was killed whilst leading his Battalion in an attack on the infamous Menin Road. His widow, Mrs Gladys Gibbs, née Morel, bought the Hotel and as a fitting memorial to her late husband opened it in 1918 as a branch of the National Children's Home. It is now Headlands School.

GLAMORGAN CLUB (LOST)

During the 19th century Penarth abounded with drinking clubs, both legal and illegal. The Glamorgan was run by Andrew Watson in the 1880s and 1890s from a building on the corner of Arcot Street and Salop Street. Now number 22 Arcot Street, it was previously the Arcot Club.

GLEBE PLACE

In the 1870s two rows of modest houses were erected between Glebe Street and the slope that runs up towards St Augustine's Church. Since the land formed the western edge of the Glebeland the thoroughfare was called Glebe Place, but later re-named King Street in 1905. When the 41 original houses were built, thirteen of them were occupied by dock labourers, later known as dockers. Two others had master stone-masons living in them, there were two blacksmiths and numerous riggers, coal-tippers and coal-trimmers. The Golden Lion, one of the town's original public houses, stood on one corner while small general stores could be found on the other three corners.

From the 1870s through to the 1890s 22 Glebe Place was the home of the St Augustine's Church Mission. Here the poor and destitute of the town could get a free meal on three days of the week and a bowl of soup on the other three days, but nothing on the Sabbath!

GLEBE STREET

This thoroughfare was the main street of the town when the original Docktown was built in the 1850s. The street formed the western boundary of the Church

---

[76] P. Carradice: Headlands School in Camera. 1991.

THE GOLDEN LION

The very popular Golden Lion.   © Diane Mead

land, or Glebeland, hence its name. The land had been given to the Prior of St Augustine's, a monastery run by an order of Black Canons in Bristol, in the 12th century. The Prior consequently became Lord of the Manor of Penarth. Between 1186 and 1191 William Saltmarsh, Prior of Bristol and Bishop of Llandaff, was Lord of the Manor and responsible for the building of the original St Augustine's Church on Penarth Head. The land was owned by the Augustine Canons until the time of the Dissolution of the Monasteries between 1536 and 1540.

When the street was originally built, the houses between the Albion Hotel and the Glebe Street arm of Chapel Lane were owned by an organisation known as the "Llantrisant Club".

78

GOLDEN GATES

A small open play area cum park located between Wordsworth Avenue and Coleridge Avenue, this name is given both to the entrances themselves and the area in general. The derivation is unknown.

GOSPEL HALL

This charming little building of most unusual design was built in Plassey Street by the Brethren and opened in 1877. They also built Hebron Hall, Cogan, in 1904 at the junction of Agnes Street and Pill Street.

GRANGE POINT

Grange Point is at the western end of the isolated promontory of the reclaimed Ely Wharf, and the site of the tree-enveloped River View House and the Victoria Wharf, both now in a state of ruin. It is best viewed from the new bridge across the River Ely.

GRASS POINT (LOST)

Before land reclamation took place in the 1850s, Grass Point was the eastern extremity of the Ely Wharf. Following reclamation, the wharf was lengthened eastwards to Mud Point. Grass Point was the site of the Anglo-American Oil Wharf, later owned by Esso, and its adjacent petrol storage tanks. The tanks have gone now, but the oil wharf, which had also operated as an iron ore wharf, can still be seen.

GRID IRON (LOST)

In the late 1870s the Penarth Ship Building and Ship Repairing Company Limited built a shipyard, slipway, jetties, railway sidings, and a grid iron on the north side of the Dock, on the southern bank of the River Ely. The grid iron, massively constructed of greenheart, was built in the river itself and alongside the shipyard. It was 374 feet long and capable of taking vessels up to 3,000 tons gross register. The company advertised special facilities for cleaning and painting vessels and for changing propellers.

The grid-iron was kept busy, particularly with work on vessels damaged in collisions, a common occurrence in such a busy dock during the boom years of the 1880s and 90s. In April 1892, for example, the SS Proudhoe Castle was steaming down Penarth Dock when it was in collision with a Swedish vessel, the Anna Theresa. Both were damaged and taken to the grid-iron for repairs to be carried out.

The grid-iron has gone now, but remnants of the grid-iron jetties can still be spotted. It was the company's proud boast in 1885 that "repairs [could be] carried out at night by the aid of electric lights[77]."

GREEN POND (LOST)

This large and very deep pond (indeed local legend claimed that it was bottomless!) was part of the Cement Works, just off Lavernock Road and alongside the narrow-gauge railway thatseparated the works from Upper Cosmeston Farm. The railway used to cross Lavernock Road and connected the Cement Works with the quarries that have now been filled in to form Cosmeston Lakes.

The Green Pond was an irresistible attraction to the Bowery Kids. It was eventually filled in, and like the now demolished Upper Cosmeston Farm, the site has been built over with a housing estate.

GROTTO

An affectionate nickname for the dungeon-like gentlemen's latrines set into the retaining wall of the lower end of Beach Hill. Although it is now all locked up and no longer in use, it can still be seen.

HAUNTED HOUSE

Number 1 Salop Street stands at the junction of this road with High Street, formerly Maughan Street. This house, which is much larger than the others in the street, was built in the 1850s. It has had a chequered life and is reputed to be haunted[78], although no names, dates or reasons are given.

During the 1860s and 1870s the house was used by various religious sects which had no premises of their own, including Baptists and Roman Catholics.

[77] Cardiff Directory, 1885.
[78] Bevan Tilney.

On 30 March, 1894, the house was raided by the Penarth Police. A notorious gang of recidivists, Cardiff's infamous 'Forty Thieves', had been prevented by the Cardiff Police from staging illegal bare-fist prize-fights in Cardiff and had transferred operations to 1 Salop Street instead. All present were arrested[79].

HALTON CLOSE

This thoroughfare is named after two small villages - Halton Lady and Halton Priors - which are about two miles from Ludlow in South Shropshire (Salop), and are part of one of the Windsor/Clive country estates.

HARRIET STREET

Harriet is a recurring name in the Windsor / Clive /Plymouth dynasty. Other Hickman, the Fifth Earl of Plymouth, had one son, Other Archer, and two daughters, Maria and Harriet. Harriet married the Honourable Robert Henry Clive, second son of the Earl of Powis on 19 June 1819. When Powis died on 20 January 1854, his widow moved to have the abeyance of the Baronetcy terminated in her favour. This was successfully achieved on 25 October 1855, and she became the Baroness Windsor[80]. Her eldest son, Robert Clive, who was born on 24 May 1824, married Lady Mary Selina Bridgeman on 20 October 1852. Their eldest daughter was christened Georgina Harriet Charlotte.

HARROGATE HOUSE

Albert Crescent was built in the 1870s and was originally known as Church Place. Number 7 was owned by a Mr Apel and was run as Harrowgate House Ladies' School, with Mrs Apel as Principal. The house next door, Glanville House, was converted into a Boy's School where Mr Apel was the Principal. In 1886,the schools merged to become the Penarth Collegiate School.

HASLAND HOUSE

During the 19th century this fine house in Victoria Road was the site of a highly regarded boys' Preparatory Boarding and Day School, whose Principal was a

[79] Penarth Observer, 1894.
[80] W. T. Williams, Windsor Monograph, ibid.

Mr Joseph Lugg. Of all the numerous 19th century private schools in the town this appears to have been one of the best. When Mr Lugg died in 1892 the school was taken over by Mr G L Wyard.

HASTINGS AVENUE

This pleasant avenue stands on land that used to belong to the Bute Family who owned the Parish of Cogan, and the name commemorates the Bute connection. Henry Hastings, the Fourth Marquess of Hastings, married Florence Cecilia Paget, youngest daughter of the Second Marquess of Anglesey, in 1864. Hastings was the son of the Second Marquess of Hastings and a cousin of the Third Marquess of Bute. When the first houses were built they were known as Shakespeare Road, but this name was soon changed.

HEAD FORT AND COASTAL BATTERY

In the 1890s plans were drawn up to build a military establishment on Penarth Head. The site was at that time an area of overgrown land that stood between the extensive grounds of the Penarth Hotel and the large gardens belonging to Upper Cliff House. The area is now the site of the Uppercliff housing estate.

The open space was used for bonfires on special occasions. Two such notable events were the festivities to mark the 21st birthday of Lord Windsor on 27 August 1878 - "as darkness set in, a ground display of fireworks - from the hill near St Augustine's Church ... and a monster bonfire was also lighted, and kept in full blaze for a considerable time"[81]. A massive bonfire was also built and lit to celebrate the relief of Mafeking in 1900[82].

The people of Penarth did not welcome the proposed 'fort'. Fears were expressed in the press that the gun explosions would have an adverse effect on the fragile cliff face. However, work was started on building the fort at the beginning of the 20th century, and included barrack-rooms, hidden gun-emplacements, lookout towers and subterranean ammunition storage dumps. Itsmajor purpose was the defence of Cardiff and Penarth Docks from waterborne attack. Uppercliff House became the Officers' Quarters and was known as Artillery House.

[81]   W. T. Williams, Windsor Monograph, ibid.
[82]   Rowlands, ibid.

During the Second World War the fort was occupied by the American Forces and together with Artillery House was used as an accommodation holding camp. It was also the site of an anti-aircraft battery. After the war ended it was used for commercial purposes, most notably a glove factory.

The grounds were a marvellous playground for the Bowery Kids, but the site was eventually cleared and a housing estate put up on the site.

The Government in power at the time the fort was planned, that it to say the late 19th century, were convinced that the French were about to attack Britain and it therefore built numerous coastal fortifications. The local press had a regular stream of letters warning of the threat from France and calling for a sea-defence. These letters encouraged the Editor to print a tongue-in-cheek article on 13 May 1892 which said: "Many local gentlemen who are entitled to write Colonel, Major, Captain etc before their names have written in that we are absolutely defenceless should an enemy send an ironclad up Channel to attack us. I hear a subscription is about to be started to defray the cost of mounting a Gatling gun and two pea shooters on the tower of the Church [St. Augustine's]; this should frighten the "darned mounseer" and would be quite as effective as the present armaments on Lavernock and the Holms[83]."

HEADLANDS SCHOOL

The school was opened on 24 October 1918 as Gibbs' House in memory of Major John Angel Gibbs[84]. Originally a National Childrens Home, it became an approved school in 1936. Up to and during the Second World War the boys attended Albert Road School. In the immediate post-war period the title Gibbs' Home was dropped and changed to Headlands School. Moves were made to establish a purpose-built school on the site, and four temporary classrooms were eventually replaced by a permanent school building and gymnasium, which was opened on 7 July 1962.

HERBERT TERRACE

During the reign of Henry VIII, William Herbert, son of Sir Richard Herbert, married Ann the daughter of Thomas, Lord Parr, and a sister of Catherine Parr, Henry VIII's last wife. William Herbert was knighted by Henry and later

[83]   Penarth Observer, 1892.
[84]   John M. Gibbs: The Morels of Cardiff. 1982.

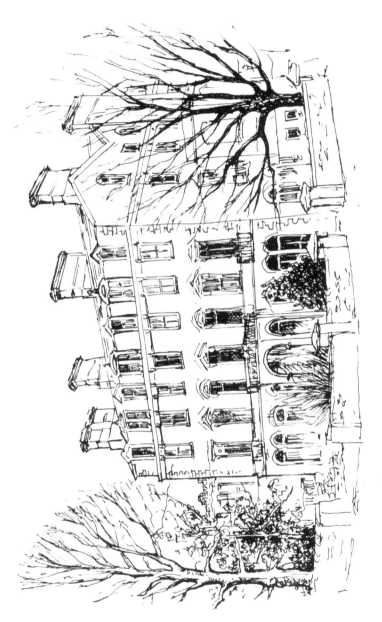

The main block at Headlands School. Built in the 1800's as the Penarth Hotel.

created Baron Herbert of Cardiff and Earl of Pembroke by Edward VII. Phillip, the Seventh Earl of Pembroke, was sixth in direct line from William and on his death his daughter Lady Charlotte Herbert inherited hisGlamorgan estate and Cardiff Castle. Lady Charlotte married Thomas, Viscount Windsor, second son of the 7th Lord Windsor, Earl of Plymouth[85].

Cogan Pill House was built by Matthew Herbert, great-great grandson of William, Baron Cardiff, in about 1554.

HEWELL STREET

This street in Cogan is named after Hewell Grange, one of the Windsor's country seats. The grange was built in 1711 on the site of an old manor house by the Second Earl of Plymouth, whose son, the third Earl, married the Welsh heiress Elizabeth Lewis. She brought to the marriage the castle and lands of St Fagans and estates which now form the nucleus of the town of Penarth.

The grange stood in 200 acres of pastoral surroundings in the beautiful Worcestershire countryside, blessed by striking contrasts of wood and water. The house was extended in 1717 by Other, Fourth Earl of Plymouth.

The grange, which as already been said was built on the site of an old manor house, stood on land previously owned by Bordesley Abbey but which had been acquired by Lord Windsor in 1542. Queen Victoria visited Hewell Grange in November 1832 when she was still a Princess[86].

HICKMAN ROAD

Thomas Hickman was the son and heir of Elizabeth, the eldest sister of Thomas, Baron Windsor of Bradenham. She had married Dixey Hickman of Kew, a nephew of Sir William Hickman of Gainsborough, Lincolnshire. This connection is also commemorated in Gainsborough Road, Cogan.

Thomas Hickman assumed the name of Windsor and was restored as Baron Windsor by Letters Patent on 6 June 1660, his uncle Thomas, Baron Windsor, having died in 1640 without issue from his union with Catherine, daughter of Edward Somerset, Earl of Worcester. Hickman was created Earl of Plymouh on 6 December 1682 and died on 10 November 1687.

[85]   W. T. Williams, Windsor Monograph, ibid.
[86]   Margaret Mabey: The Windsors of Hewell. 1984.

HIGHLAND CRESCENT (LOST)

This charming terrace of 13 cottages cut into the southern edge of the Penarth Ridge originally joined Plassey Street and Windsor Road. It has been known as Hill Terrace since 1897. The cottages were built in 1892 when the original plan was to build just eight. This was increased by another five after numerous impassioned representations were made to the Local Board by thebuilder, Mr H Smith.

HIGH LEVEL SIDINGS (LOST)

When the Dock was being built between 1859 and 1865, extensive sidings were laid out to serve the coal-tips, of which there were fourteen in all, located on the south side of the Dock. The sidings stretched in an east-west direction from Cogan to the Dock Basin, and from the foot of the man-made escarpment north towards the man-made cliff directly above the south side of the Dock. In the 1860s there were plans to make the eastern end of the sidings the site of a station being proposed by the Taff Vale Railway to serve the Penarth Hotel, which they owned. This idea, however, was soon abandoned.

The sidings, which were also known as the Upper Level, had railway lines running out to the tips. The empty coal-trucks were returned along deep, sunken lines. They have been lost now as a result of recent development work in the area.

HIPPODROME (LOST)

Solomon Andrews' Large Hall in Albert Road underwent numerous changes of name during its chequered existence. During the 1920s it was known as the Hippodrome, and was the venue of many productions of operettas under the guidance of the highly respected Rupert Batten. The site is now part of the Royal Mail's Albert Road complex.

The hall suffered serious fire damage on 11 May 1929.

HOLE IN THE WALL

This is the affectionate name given to the alfresco gentleman's toilet set into the retaining wall just north of the Windsor Road railway bridge. Originally, and indeed until only recently, it comprised a beautifully ornate cast-iron urinal, but this has now been replaced with modern materials. It was one of the many alfresco urinals around the town, most, alas, now lost. Others included the one at the top of Dock Subway Road, the one outside the former Mission to Seamen in Cogan, and the one outside the Ship Hotel.

HOLLIES (LOST)

The Hollies was an excellent example of the many grand mansions that Penarth used to be able to boast. This beautiful building stood at the top of Beach Road (previously Penarth Terrace) in extensive, well laid out gardens surrounded by trees and a massive stone boundary wall constructed of local stone. The house, which was built in the 1860s, was the home of George Taylor, a coal factor.

It was ultimately demolished and replaced by Albany Court. The massive boundary wall and some of the trees are all that are left now.

HOLMESDALE PLACE

In 1778 Other Hickman, the Fifth Earl of Plymouth, born 1751, married Sarah, daughter and heir of Andrew, Lord Archer. On Hickman's death, his wife the Dowager Countess married William Pitt, Viscount Holmesdale. On Sarah's death Holmesdale married the Dowager Countess, widow of the Sixth Earl of Plymouth.

HONG KONG (LOST)

Salop House stands at the junction of Arcot Street and Salop Street on the site of an earlier substantial building which had been erected in the 1850s and which was similar in design to the Plymouth Hotel. The building had a grand Bath stone facade.

The original use of the building is as yet unknown, but as it had extensive cellars and a large amount of stabling to the rear, it is likely it was a public house. This is especially so when one remembers that the only large buildings in early Penarth were either churches or public houses. The Hong Kong may have been the original name of the Royal Oak.

Between the 1870s and the 1890s it was the Liberal Club, when it was licensed for drinking and gambling.

From 5 October 1894 until 1905 it was home to the town's first library. In 1905 it became a tenement building with a general shop on the ground floor. In 1911 the ground floor was converted into a laundry that was owned and run by Sydney Wills. From 1913 until 1916 the ground floor was used as both a laundry and a shop run by Mrs Jenkins. From 1920 until at least 1929 the building was occupied by Sam Chick who advertised 'boarding accommodation', although a shop was still being operated from the premise. The shop was owned variously by Mrs Jenkins, Mr Ed Grey and Mr F Herbert. Its years as a laundry may have something to do with the name Hong Kong, although there is no evidence of any Chinese connection.

During the Second World War it was used to billet servicemen. After the war it became derelict and was a wonderful playground for the Bowery Boys. It was finally demolished and council flats built on the site.

The derivation of the name Hong Kong is unknown.

HOUSE OF MERCY (LOST)

Known until its recent demolition as Llandaff House and used as an annexe for the University of Wales, this very large, rather austere and forbidding house was built in the early 1880s. A Diocesan Institution, the House of Mercy for Llandaff Cathedral was used to house penitents, many of them fallen women from the Diocese.

The house continued a historical link with Llandaff that had started in the 12th century when Saltmarsh, the Bishop of Llandaff, was Lord of the Manor of Penarth.

When first built the house stood in splendid isolation surrounded by fields, the nearest buildings being Cornerswell Farm to the north-west and Cwrt-y-Vil House (Raithwaite) to the south.

HYDRAULIC HOUSE AND ENGINE HOUSE (LOST)

When Penarth Dock was at its zenith there were about one hundred buildings on the dock-sides and its periphery, ranging in size from small sheds and lodges used by boatmen and berthing-men right up to the imposing Custom House and perhaps the most important buildings of all, the massive Hydraulic House and its attendant Engine House. The massive Hydraulic House built of local red brick had numerous large arched windows and with its tall brick chimney it must have looked like an industrial cathedral. This was accentuated by the stone-built Engine House which was built against the eastern end of the Hydraulic House. The Engine House had three large gables, impressive arched windows and a tall, windowed tower all in the Italianate style -a side chapel, perhaps, to the industrial cathedral of the Hydraulic House.

The buildings produced the pressurized water needed to power the machinery operating the massive lock gates. There were four such gates in all - two sets of sea-lock gates and two sets dividing the Dock Basin from the Main Dock. It also provided power for the cranes, coal tips etc. Everything was powered by water supplied from the reservoir at Llandough above Penarth Road at what is today Cogan Pill Road.

On 28 October 1892, a burst water pipe badly affected the water supply. Panic ensued, but a potential disaster was averted when the Dock Master managed to get the sea lock-gates closed again with the last remnants of power available[87].

IMPERIAL WHARF (LOST)

The full title was the Imperial Wharf and Landing Steps, and it was located about 150 yards further up the River Ely than the No. 2 Victoria Wharf.

JACOB'S LADDER (LOST)

During the Second World War the dock and the town were taken over by the American Armed Forces, and for all intents and purposes it became an American garrison. Scores of houses and buildings were requisitioned, and numerous camps set up with the ubiquitous Quonset hut, the American equivalent of our Nissen hut. Northcliff House (Cliff Villa), together with its extensive grounds and woodlands, was one such property and to shorten the route to the dock a massive wooden stairway was built from the side of the Custom House (previously the site of the stables for the Penarth Head Inn) up to the top of the cliff. The stairway soon became known as Jacob's Ladder.

With the cessation of hostilities in 1945, the stairway was demolished, although the last of the buildings built by the American forces around Northcliff Wood were only finally demolished just before work began on the building of Mariner's Heights.

[87] Penarth Observer, October 1892.

JENKINSVILLE

Jenkinsville was originally the name of a row of houses built before the Second World War at the point where Clive Place meets St. Augustine's Crescent. The row is named after the man who built them, although the name is also used for the council flats on the other side of the road, and indeed for the whole local area in general.

JOHNSTONE'S WHARF (LOST)

The location of this wharf in the Ely Tidal Harbour is yet to be pinpointed, although it could well have been one of the many wharfs now lost due to demolition.

In March 1892 the SS Sir Walter Raleigh was long overdue on a voyage from Philadelphia to Dunkirk. It was loaded with a cargo of maize, and had been battered across the Atlantic by continuous storms and gales. The ship's engines eventually failed, whereupon it was driven into the Bay of Biscay. Fortunately, it was spotted and taken in tow by the Ninian Stuart, one of the ships belonging to Morel's extensive fleet. The vessel was towed to Penarth "and its cargo unloaded at Johnstone's Wharf, Ely Harbour"[88].

JUBILEE HALL (LOST)

The name lives on in today's Jubilee Lane, but the original Jubilee Hall was a large public hall built in the gardens of numbers 1 and 2 Albert Crescent in the 1880s. Jubilee Hall was owned by Albert Cope, a Bristol Channel Pilot who lived at 1 Albert Crescent. His father was reputedly the town's first tobacconist, also called Albert Cope, who had a shop in Glebe Street.

The hall was used for meetings and concerts and by various religious groups who had no premises of their own. The Welsh Calvinists held services there, and Dame Clara Novello gave two concerts at the hall in the 1890s to raise funds for the building of the Bethania Calvinist Chapel in Hickman Road.

Jubilee Hall, Cope's house and 2 Albert Crescent, which used to house a small preparatory school, Varteg House, run by Mr and Mrs Jones, were all demolished to make way for the building of Albert Road Wesleyan Church, which was opened on 29 May 1907 by Mrs John Cory.

[88] Penarth Observer, 1892.

KENDRICK HOUSE

This house in Victoria Road was home to yet another of the town's many schools in the nineteenth century. This one catered for Young Ladies and was owned by Mr John Wallis and run by the Misses Wallis as co-principals. One of their advertisements boasted of there being "Professors in attendance for special branches". Kendrick House was advertised as a "Boarding and Day School".

KINEMA

Penarth's first custom-built cinema was the Windsor Kinema which was constructed during the First World War for the Willmore Brothers. Earlier, during the 1880s and 90s, the site had housed a large iron hall, originally a Congregational Church, where Dr Joseph Parry gave a sacred concert in aid of the Organ Fund in March 1892 before a large audience who had paid one shilling (two shillings for the better seats) for their tickets.

The premises then became Solomon Andrews's Windsor Hall before being turned into a Drill Hall for the Third Volunteer Battalion of the 2/7th Welsh Regiment (Cyclists). This battalion was to see some of the bloodiest action in the Great War. Their exploits, incidentally, are commemorated by a plaque on one of the plinths erected outside Cardiff City Hall.

The Kinema premises were finally acquired by the Wilmore Brothers in 1912, and used as a cinema until its demolition and the building of the what was for those times an ultra modern building, also known as the Kinema.

KNOWBURY AVENUE

Knowbury was another of the estates in Shropshire held by the Windsor Family. It formed part of the larger Oakley Park Estate just outside Ludlow.

KYMIN

The Kymin is the name of a large house, one of the town's oldest buildings in fact, which was built between 1790 and 1810. But it also applies to the general area surrounding the house, which mainly comprises an extensive steep-sided densely wooded dingle.

The Kymin is built on the site of an earlier building, Kimmin Farm. The farm was occupied in 1700 by Gwenllian Evans. The first recorded occupants of the later house appear to have been John Minchin, an Irishman described in the 1841 Census as an Army Captain (Retired). By the time of the 1871 Census we find James Sidney Batchelor, brother of the famous John Batchelor, recorded as the occupant. The house is now owned by the Local Authority.

The Kymin dingle used to be intersected by a vigorous stream, now culverted, that drained from the Penarth Ridge. G. O. Pierce suggests the name Kymin is derived from Le Comon or the Comen, meaning 'common land'. This seems unlikely, however, as there appears to have been no common land in the Parish of Penarth, and common land is rarely, if ever, found in dingles, dells or low lying land. Most common land, especially in this area of Wales, is on raised land, usually a plateau, as is the case with Dinas Powis Common, Cadoxton, etc. Again common land was usually found near habitations, so the obvious site for common land in the Penarth Parish would have been in the vicinity of what is today the town roundabout or Victoria Square.

Kymin appears to derive from a combination of the old Celtic 'Ki", meaning a stream, and 'minni', the old Norse word for the mouth of a stream. Before urbanization took place, the southern end of today's Kymin, at the bottom of Beach Hill, formed the confluence of three streams. This would have been the nearest available source of fresh water for the Vikings living on the Flat Holm.

There are numerous recorded versions of the name which support this hypothesis that the name Kymin is derived from Ki and Minni. Other versions include Cymin, Cymmyn, Kimming, Minning, Kimmin and Kemmin.

LA SLYME (lost)

The earliest references to La Slyme appear to be those found in early Norman ecclesiastical and Court records, particularly those concerning fishing rights and dues. The name applied to the vast area of mud between Penarth and Cardiff which was later known as Penarth Flats.

LAVERNOCK

The earliest reference to Lavernock appears to be the 13th century Lawernek. Since that time there have been more than 20 different spellings recorded, including Lannock (1537), Larnott (1596), Llavernock (1642), and Lavernoc (1794). Its derivation is difficult to establish and there are two main theories. The first is that the name might be derived from St. Lawrence, who is

92

commemorated in the church at Lavernock Point, and certainly one early name for the area was Sain Lawrens (1566).

Another theory propounded by Paterson[89] is that the name is Norse in origin. The Vikings had a propensity for giving prominent coastal features animal or anatomical names. Compare for example Rani (Ranny) - hog's snout. Paterson suggests a combination of the old Norse lag, meaning a layer or stratum, and nakki or neck, a word that was sometimes used to describe a rounded coast projecting out into the sea with a steep slope or cliff behind. Both would usefully describe the area around Lavernock Point.

LE BRODEFIORD (LOST)

This name, which enjoyed common currency during Norman times, was used on a number of occasions in attempts to determine 'ownership' of the fishing rights on the foreshore. Le Brodefiord described the stretch of foreshore and sea between Lavernock Point and Penarth Head. The derivation can again be traced to the Viking presence in the area, which was continuous between the 8th century and the Norman occupation. 'Brode' translates as broad, while fiord means inlet - an apt description for the broad stretch of water between the cliffs and foreshore at Penarth and the offshore sandbanks.

Directly across the Channel, between Weston and Clevedon, lie sand banks called Langford Grounds. The late Graham Farr suggests Langford comes from the old Norse Longfiord.[90]

LEVEL CROSSING (LOST)

The town's only level crossing ran between Windsor Place and West Terrace. Before the railway line was laid in 1878 this site formed part of a path that stretched down from the Glebeland, across the fields where Arcot Street and Windsor Road now stand, before linking with another path that led from Bute Cottage to join up with the former Parish Road, now Stanwell Road. The present Bute Lane follows the same route as the old path.

The level crossing was opened in 1878 and closed when a footbridge was constructed in the 1890s. The footbridge was demolished when the present footbridge at the Dingle Halt was constructed in 1904.

[89] Paterson, ibid.
[90] Farr, Ordnance Survey 1878/9.

In 1892 Annie Davies, a young girl of 14 who was born in Gloucester, was employed as a maid at the newly-built 88 Windsor Road. She was accused by the lady of the house of stealing a pound. A violent argument ensued and Annie was given a month's notice. Deeply distressed, she ran out of the house, still in her uniform, and was fatally struck by the 8.17 a.m. train to Cardiff as she dashed across the level crossing[91].

In the early 1890s numerous complaints were received by the Local Board from ladies who had had their dresses torn on barbed wire put up near the level crossing. Mr Rowlands states that a level crossing existed near Finch's Laundry which used to operate from the west end of Grove Terrace[92].

LIFEBOAT HOUSE

The town's first Lifeboat House was built on a site now covered by the southern wing of Penarth Yacht Club, and was opened in 1861. The first lifeboat was the George Gay, subsequently renamed the Baroness Windsor. At the formal opening of Penarth Dock on 10 June 1865, the lifeboat was fourth in the procession of vessels entering the dock. Lady Mary Windsor Clive christened the lifeboat by "throwing a bottle of wine at it". Its first call to official duty had come on 3 December 1863 when the full-rigged ship Jupiter and the barque Ellings collided in Penarth Roads.

The George Gay II (which was in service from March 1868 until 1875) and the Joseph Denman I (November 1875 - 1881) were also kept at the Lifeboat House. In December 1881 delivery was taken of a larger vessel, the Joseph Denman II, and this was kept moored at the entrance to Penarth Docks. Between 1883 and 1884 a new Lifeboat House and slipway were built under Penarth Head (see ANDERSONS). The Joseph Denman II was on station until 1898 when it was replaced by the Joseph Denman III.

At a meeting of the Royal National Institution's Committee of Management on 9 November 1905, the decision was taken to close the Penarth Station. The last call to service from the original Lifeboat House came on 28 December 1900 when the Italian barque Zefiro was in collision with the Nova Scotia registered King's Country. Nine men and the captain's wife were saved from the Zefiro[93].

---

[91]   Penarth Observer, 1892.
[92]   Rowlands, ibid.
[93]   G. Farr, ibid.

Nothing remains of the Lifeboat House, although until 1994 a section of its slipway could still be seen. This disappeared when work started on the Cardiff Barrage.

LIFEBOATS

The George Gay, a light 30 ft long Peake Second Class vessel rowing six oars single banked had been delivered by rail on 28 January 1861. The vessel was named after her donor. The George Gay II, a slightly larger boat at 32 ft long, arrived in March 1868 and had ten oar positions.

Delivery was taken of the Joseph Denman in November 1875. This was a 30 ft self-righting boat rowing eight oars. The boats were a gift from the Honourable Mrs Denman and named in memory of her late husband, Admiral the Honourable Joseph Denman.

The Joseph Denman II, a 37 ft, twelve-oared self-righting vessel was taken delivery of in December 1881, while the Joseph Denman III arrived in 1898. This boat was the same size as the Joseph Denman II[94].

LIMEKILN COTTAGES (LOST)

The three dwellings known as the Limekiln Cottages used to stand halfway down the right hand side of Dock Subway Road. The date of their construction is not known, although they are shown on early maps of Penarth[95]. In later years they were overshadowed by one of the massive heaps or banks of spoil dumped from the lime-pits and the stone quarry.

The cottages were still inhabited in the late 1920s by three families - the Barnetts, the Prices and the Wests. The cottages, or at least their ruins, were lost when the Billybanks site was landscaped in preparation for the building of the Council flats.

The site of the cottages is approximately where the row of garages just to the west of the flats stand today.

LINDENS

This grand house, thankfully still standing albeit facing an uncertain future, was the home of Thomas and Susanna Morel and their five children from 1880

[94]   Cardiff Directory, 1929.
[95]   O/S (various).

95

onwards. Set in extensive gardens, the house stands at the junction of Beach Lane and Bradford Place and until recently was used as a Children's Home. The Lindens still retains much of its original grandeur, including a large billiard room that was added on in the summer of 1892. Unfortunately, the unique entrance lodge, built to resemble an Alpine chalet, has now been demolished. The design of the lodge, which was constructed at a later date than the main house, may have been influenced by a visit Thomas Morel paid to Switzerland in July, 1891.

Thomas Morel died on 7 October 1903. The house was then occupied by A Beasley until the 1920s when Lt Col. J. H. R. Downes-Powell JP, the Chairman of the Penarth Urban District Council, took up residence and remained at the Lindens until the Second World War.

LLANDOUGH

St. Dochdwy (Dochan, Docheu, or Docunni, also known as the Abbot Cyngar, crossed the Severn Sea from Glastonbury and is reputed to have landed near a "high mountain" (could this have been Penarth Head?), from where he moved up the River Ely and on to Llandough Pill - lost when the railway embankment was built in the 1850s - before climbing up through a steep, wooded hill along the banks of a stream. When he reached the top of the hill he liked the "... pleasing prospect" and established first a hermitage as an anchorite, then a monastic foundation, and later a school. It is from him that the present day Llandough takes its name.

The monastery had 12 monks or canons, and in its heyday was, along with Llantwit Major and Llancarvan, one of the three principal Celtic monastic communities established by the early Celtic Saints (who also included Cadoc, Cadfan, Cornelius, and Gildas).

Before the demolition of the old Llandough School (opened in 1878), an inscription to St. Dochdwy could be seen cut into the stone above the main doorway.

Other early spellings included Llandachôn (1100), Landoche (1200), Llandocw (1300), Llandogh by Pennarth (1542), etc.

LLOYDS SIGNAL STATION (LOST)

Before the advent of ship-to-shore radio, contact was made with vessels by means of semaphore. This involved either hand-held flags or signalling apparatus similar to the old railway signals and involving a series of hoisted flags and lamps.

During the 19th century, the Bristol Channel was perhaps the busiest waterway in the world and Penarth Roads might have as many as 500 vessels lying at anchor at any one time[96]. Communications were therefore of paramount importance, and Lloyd's built a signal station on Penarth Head. It was opened on 25 October 1895 and was also used as an accommodation block from where a round the clock watch was maintained. Further signalling devices were installed by Lloyds at the end of the Pier, again in 1895, as well as at Lavernock Point.

The Penarth Head has probably been used as a lookout and signalling point since man first took to the water. Bevan suggests that "Penarth Head was used as a beacon from the earliest days, with the Garth being the next one"[97].

The station is now a private residence, Monkstone, at the seaward end of Penarth Head Lane. The garden still contains a few of the original signalling fittings, reminders of the house's past association with maritime activities.

LOCOMOTIVE SHEDS (LOST)

By the 1880s the export of Welsh steam coal from Penarth had increased at an astonishing rate. The export figures for 1870 were 900,000 tons, more than doubling to 2,000,000 tons by 1882, and up yet further to 2,274,003 tons in 1883. The Dock Extension was completed in 1884, whereupon exports rose to over 3,000,000 tons a year.

By 1878 Penarth had also become the southern terminus for passenger traffic on the Taff Vale Railway. There was a need for locomotive sheds to cater for the various mineral, passenger and shunting engines. The Taff Vale Railway built large sheds and numerous ancillary buildings on the site of Dock Cottages, which had at that time recently been demolished. The sheds opened in 1887 with accommodation for 25 steam engines[98].

The fall off in dock trade in the 1920s led to the sheds being officially closed in February 1929, although records show that they were still working until April 1929. They were finally demolished in the 1930s. Tesco's car park now covers the site, but before it was tarmacked over much of the remains of the sheds and their ancillary buildings could still be seen in the undergrowth.

[96]   R. Thorne, ibid.
[97]   Bevan. Unpublished monograph. Ibid.
[98]   Mountford & Spinks, ibid.

The sheds were also known as the Engine Sheds. They were 120 ft long by 45 ft wide, solidly constructed of stone and had a handsome gabled roof. The ancillary buildings included coal stores, blacksmiths' forges, a machine shop, pump house, boilerhouse, stores and offices and, of course, the famous Black Tank.

LOWER FORD (LOST)

This name is another reminder of the Viking presence in and around Penarth and is derived from the Old Norse Lower Fiord/Fjord. The name was in common usage right up until the building of the dock. It refers to the area off Penarth Head, just north of the Patch, a shingle bank of mud separating the mouths of the rivers Ely and Taff[99]

LOWER LAYER (LOST)

An early name which we know dates back from at least Norman times, Lower Layer used to describe the mud flats and a section of the River Taff in front of the Penarth Railway Hotel (the Red House)[100].

LOWER MARSH (LOST)

Before the dock was excavated, the Penarth Ridge sloped gently down to extensive tidal fields that stretched from the Cwtsh-y-Cwm westwards along the southern bank of the River Ely towards Cogan. The area between Cwtsh-y-Cwm and the smaller Pill fed by a stream from the Billy Banks was known as the Lower Marsh. All disappeared with the building of the dock in the middle of the last century.

LOWER PENARTH HALT

This Taff Vale Railway station was opened in 1897 and called simply Lower Penarth. It was renamed Lower Penarth Halt on 30 September 1935. The two platforms and the associated station buildings stood roughly where Charteris Close is today, about a mile from the Penarth Town station. The station was

[99] Smythe, ibid.
[100] Mountford & Spinks: The Taff Vale Lines to Penarth. 1993.

opened on 2 January 1897 amid great ceremony, a private opening for members of the nearby Glamorgan Golf Club, followed by the official public opening on Monday, 18 February 1897[101]. The station closed to passenger services on 14 July 1954, whereupon the largest station building was turned into a private residence.

LUDLOW STREET

Ludlow Street is named after a town in Shropshire where the Windsor-Clive family held numerous large estates.

LYCEUM THEATRE (LOST)

The Lyceum was the town's only bona fide theatre and during the 19th century it stood at the intersection of Glebe Street, Salop Street and Salop Place. Its very name conjures up images of Penarth's own stage-door Johnnies, hansom cabs, opera cloaks and flickering naphtha lamps. And then there were the performers themselves - archetypal moustache-twirling Victorian mountebanks, actor-managers and dancers, etc.

The theatre was licensed to seat 650 patrons, and in 1891 it was being operated on a temporary licence by a Mr and Mrs Horton of Ferndale, previously of Cadoxton. The theatre had at an earlier time been owned by a Mr Johnson. But by 1892 it would appear the theatre was not enjoying the patronage it sought. A correspondent wrote in the local press: "Tuesday, 18 March 1892. It always affords me great pain to see the crowd who nightly travel by train to Cardiff to fill their theatres ..... when they have on their doorstep the Lyceum...... I noticed Mr Irving in the Dress Circle last Tuesday"[102]. Then again later in the same year we find: "Lost, stolen or strayed, a first class provincial theatre. Entering from the Dress Circle there was a strong smell of fried fish ... I suppose our Lyceum has been ruined like everything else in this benighted town by lack of support[103]".

The theatre was demolished and large shops put up on the site.

For some unknown reason, the theatre is not mentioned in any previous books about Penarth, including official Victorian guide books so the dates of its building and demolition are therefore yet to be established.

[101]   Mountford & Spinks, ibid.
[102]   Penarth Observer.
[103]   Penarth Observer.

MARINA

The Bijou at the seaward end of the Pier was burned down on the night of Monday, 3 August 1931. Fortunately the New Pavilion had been officially opened just a few years earlier on 18 May 1929 by Mrs A Pertwee. Miss Doris Pawley had sung 'Land of Hope and Glory' and 'Rock of Ages' during the opening celebrations.

The Pavilion was used for concerts and dances until Easter Monday 1932, when Messrs. Cooper and Wright, who had formed The Lyceum (Penarth) Limited, opened a cinema. Their first programme showed two films, 'Bad Girl' and 'Two Crowded Hours'. The Pavilion Cinema closed its doors in June 1933.

In 1934 a group of local businessmen turned the venue into a dance hall. A dance floor was laid and the Marina was opened in October 1934. The building, with its distinctive architecture, is now known as the Commodore.

MARINE CLUB (LOST)

The Marine Club was another of the many drinking dens that sprang up in the docktown during the 19th century. The club was based at 13 Maughan Place, now Maughan Terrace, and had a notorious reputation, being much frequented by ladies "of a particular persuasion".

MARINE HOTEL

This public house was much patronized by dock workers and the crews of vessels moored both in the dock itself and off the dock entrance. The pub used to stand at the seaward end of the Dock Buildings. In the 1881 Census it was shown as the Penarth Pier Head Tap, with a Marion A. Millar, a native of Holland, recorded as manageress of the Dock Bar. It closed just before the outbreak of the Second World War.

The public house has long been demolished, although the cellars are still there, as is the boundary wall and for some unknown reason the granite steps that used to lead up to both the bar and the smoke room. They now, of course, lead nowhere.

MASONIC HALL (LOST)

The town's first Masonic Hall appears to have been at 47/48 Windsor Road, having been established in the late 1880s. By the early 1890s the Masons were meeting in premises in Station Approach. The present Masonic Hall in Stanwell Road was built on the site of the town's original cricket and football ground in the late 1930s.

MATTHEWS YOUNG LADIES SCHOOL (LOST)

A Mr George Matthews ran a private school for young ladies for four short years between 1890 and 1894 from a house known as the Lindens, 4 Albert Crescent.

MAUGHAN PLACE (LOST)

This was the original name for what is today's Maughan Terrace. Early residents included W. Nell, the brewer, whose Eagle Brewery stood behind the public house now known as The Buccaneer in Cardiff. Nell shared the house with his son, R.F. Nell, (a surgeon, who went on to become the town's first Medical Officer), his wife, and their two servants. Maughan was the name of an agent to the Windsor/Clive family.

MAUGHAN STREET

This street was also named after the Windsor's agent Maughan (see above). During the 1850s and right up to the 1890s the street stretched from the Police Station as far as the junction with John Street. One section was named High Street in around 1890, and Maughan Street subsequently became Queens Road in honour of the Queen's Coronation in 1953.

An early resident was Peter Bethal. In the 1861 Census he is shown as a Town Missionary, born in Flint, North Wales. By the time of the 1871 Census we find Joshua Parford Vesper, an artist from Tavistock, listed as having lodgings in Maughan Street, where he lived with his daughter, aged 12, and two sons aged seven and ten.

MELIDEN ROAD

Meliden is a picturesque village in Flintshire and the name of one of the estates that used to be owned by the Windsor-Clive family. Meliden Road runs along a line that divided the town's original cricket and football ground from

Crossline's Nursery. The Pavilion stood where Meliden House stands today on the corner of Stanwell Road and the Grandstand stood where Meliden Road Joins Cornerswell Road.

MIDDLEWERE (LOST)

In the 12th century, numerous weirs were built on the River Ely to support fisheries. These were owned by the Monks of Margam Abbey and leased out. The weirs were often mentioned in Court cases, including one in 1456. The exact location of Middlewere is as yet unknown.[104]

'MILKIES'

The Milkies was a popular nickname for the wood which had in earlier days been known as both Adam's Wood and Coed-y-Hebog. The derivation of the name 'Milkies', however, is uncertain. Certainly there was a smallholding at the northern end of the wood and this may well have included some cows kept for milk. Remains of various lean-to's and sheds can still be seen on the site. Another possible explanation is that the first house built in Agnes Street in roughly the 1880s was the home of John Griffith, a dairyman. By the time the row of eight houses had been completed and numbered in the 1890s, Mr Griffith's house had become number 2. By 1903 the house was occupied by Edward Morgan, another dairyman. It is possibly that until the Second World War both had kept their cows in the smallholding, hence the name Milkies.

MISS DAVIES'S LADIES SCHOOL (LOST)

This was another of the many small schools that mushroomed around the town between 1870 to 1900. This one, with the eponymous Miss Davies as its Principal, taught young ladies from its premises at 30 Westbourne Road.

MISSION TO SEAMEN (LOST)

Whilst convalescing at Clevedon in 1835, the Rev. Dr. John Ashley noted the hundreds of vessels anchored in Penarth Roads. His young son, meanwhile, had noticed the sun glinting on windows in buildings out on Flat Holm and was

---

[104] Paterson, ibid.

reputed to have asked his father, "How can those people go to Church"[105]. The idea of a floating ministry was born in the good Reverend's mind. In 1839 he had the Eirene (Peace) built at Pill along the lines of a pilot boat with a main cabin that could be converted to hold a hundred people. The vessel was used to work the area between Bristol and Penarth. The first ship Ashley visited was a man-of-war at anchor in the King Road off the mouth of the Bristol Avon, which had been swinging at anchor for six months after coming from Spain. He also visited vessels at anchor and the communities on both the Flat and the Steep Holms.

A Mission building, a small iron shed, was erected in 1865 on the south bank of the River Ely at Penarth Dock, where it was used as a chapel and reading rooms. On 19 October 1878 Lord Windsor, accompanied by two of his sisters, Lady Mary Windsor Clive and the Honourable Georgina Clive, opened a new Mission to Seamen with Reading Rooms on the site where the Bute Basin joinedthe Dock[106]. The building cost £800. It would have cost more, but local merchants agreed to supply the materials at cost price. The building was a substantial two-storeyed affair built of local red and yellow brick. The Rector of Penarth, the Reverend C. Parsons, conducted the inaugural service. The bells of St. Augustine's rang throughout the day, and all the vessels in the Basin and the Dock were bedecked with flags and bunting.

The opening service was followed by a sumptuous lunch held in a warehouse belonging to Messrs. Alexander and Company. 170 people sat down to eat, the meal prepared and served by Mr R Wain of the Royal Hotel, Cardiff, and the Penarth Hotel. James Ware, JP, the shipowner who was living at Briarbank, Beach Road, at the time, presided. The Mission was demolished to make way for the Dock Housing Estate and Marina developments.

The town's last Mission to Seamen was housed in the large single storey building now used by the Cogan Old Age Pensions at the entrance to Cogan Station Approach.

MONKEY POLE

At various times the Penarth Coastguard had a training pole sited on the cliff, and later on the foreshore. It was used for the men to practice their Rocket and Life-saving drills and was affectionately known as the Monkey Pole.

---

[105] G. Farr: Somerset Harbours. 1954.
[106] WW. P. Williams. Windsor Monograph. 1878.

On 28 April 1893 the local Coastguard held their annual inspection which on this occasion was carried out by none other than Prince Louis Battenburg, father of Lord Louis Mountbatten. He inspected the Coastguard Cottages and Station buildings - the Watch Tower, the Rocket House, and so on, before watching the men being put through their paces with cutlass and rocket drills.

MONKSTONE ROCK

The Monkstone Rock is a shelf of rock between Penarth and Weston that is exposed at low tide and dries out to ten feet in depth. A small lighthouse has marked this danger to vessels sailing to and from Bristol. The derivation is at yet unknown. The surrounding areas on both sides of the Bristol Channel, however, have numerous monastic connections. There were small monasteries on both Flat Holm and Steep Holm, and others at Llandough and Woodspring Abbey. St. Barruc (the same Finbarr who is the Patron Saint of Cork) was drowned after leaving nearby Flat Holm to sail to Barry.

The light, a beacon 51.5 feet high, was erected on the Monkstone Rock on 12 August 1854. Alderman Trounce noted "To mariners this was a relief as the rock was most dangerous to navigation, many lives and many vessels were lost there."[107]

MORRISTOWN

In the 1890s two rows of stone houses were built on either side of the newly-constructed Cefn Mably. They were named after the builder, Mr W L Morris, a member of the Local Board. The name now applies to the general area around the Cefn Mably.

MUD POINT (LOST)

Before the Ely Tidal Harbour was built, the eastern extremity of the land, what is now Ely Wharf, was known as Grass Point. It was extended eastwards by tipping on a long mud promontory that dried out at low water known as Mud Point. The land thus reclaimed is now the site of the Penarth Motor Boat and

[107] W. J. Trounce: Cardiff in the Fifties. (1918)

Sailing Club's boatyard, slipway and club house, as well as the Grangetown entrance to the River Ely Subway.

The point was built with a southerly curve to protect vessels using the Tidal Harbour against the easterly winds. To protect the re-claimed land, a large sea wall was built. This used to stretch from the Penarth Railway Hotel (the Red House), around Mud Point, then right up the river, past Grass Point. Sections of the wall can still be found by the diligent searcher.

NATIONAL SCHOOL

As the dock town grew during the middle of the last century, there were ever increasing demands for a school to be built. Any Penarth child who did attend school had to walk to Llandough to the Dame School that had been opened there on the corner of Lewis Road in 1821, and which can still be seen today. To meet the demands for a National School, a Church of England school was opened in 1863, which was known as St. Augustine's School. It was built at the junction of Maughan Street (now High Street) and Plassey Street, at a cost of £1,400 which was borne by Baroness Windsor. It could accommodate 175 children and the Head Teacher's house was built alongside. Both the school and the house remain virtually untouched by modernization and stand as classic examples of the genre.

NEKE (LOST)

This fishery, one of many in the River Ely, owes its name to the Old English word nakki, which means a neck of land, i.e. a narrow piece of land with water on both sides. It may well have been one of the many ox-bow bends in existence before the river was straightened out and may have been another name for Grange Point. G.O. Pierce[108] dates a reference to the Neke back to 1492. Robert, Earl of Gloucester, granted a fishery to the Bishop of Llandaff in 1126, which could well have related to the same site.

NIWERE (LOST)

Ever since the time of the Norman occupation, which had been spearheaded in this area of South Wales by Robert Fitzhamon who had landed with his

---

[108]   G. O. Pierce. ibid.

HEADMASTER'S HOUSE

© Diane Mead

The Head Teacher's house at the National School, St. Augustine's, Church School in Plassey Street opened 1863.

expedition at Penarth in 1093, the River Ely had been portioned off and leased for fishing. (See Middlewere and Neke). Weirs were built to enable fishing at all times, irrespective of the state of the tide, and litigation over fishing rights were a common occurrence, especially in the 12th to 15th centuries.

The Niwere, or New Weir, was in the manor of Cogan near the Neke, so it could have been between Grange Point and the river bank below Cogan Pill House. A weir on the River Ely just above Leckwith Bridge was not demolished until 1941.

NORDEN (LOST)

As early as 1290[109] and again in the early 14th century, we find a reference to a farm known as Norden. The derivation would appear to be from the Old English words noro meaning north or northern and dun, a hill. The site of this early farm is not known, although the name suggests a site to the north of the parish, up on the Ridge. In 1700 there is a record of a farm known as Northlands, although again its exact location is unknown.

NORRIS ROW

Mr Norris was a builder and a member of the Local Board in the last century. In the 1890s he contested all four of the town's wards and won two of them. He was also a well-respected benefactor who helped the local poor. Norris Row consists of five small houses, including Althorne Cottage at the bottom of Plassey Street, between the lane and Holy Nativity Church. George Lewis Norris died in December 1893.

NORTHCLIFF

This large beautiful house, with its grand glass domed ballroom, stood in extensive landscaped and wooded grounds that are now the site of the Northcliffe flats and Mariner's Heights. It was built in the 1840s as Cliff Villa. The house had a tower built on it in the 1860s by John Batchelor, which was immediately demolished on the orders of the Taff Vale Railway and the Windsor Estate. A unique two-storey billiard room and observation room, as well as a summer house, were also built into the cliff, topped by a large

[109]   G. O. Pierce. ibid.

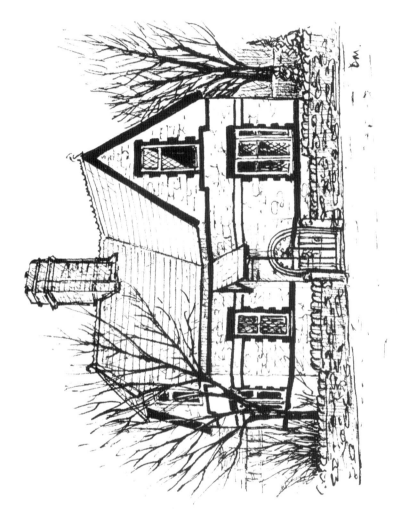

Northcliff Cottage, formerly the lodge to North Cliff.

balustrade and terrace, the whole thing supported by a massive sea wall. The cliff house and the wall can still be seen.

Northcliff house was demolished in the late 1960s. Before the present flats and Mariner's Heights were built, a length of a dried out water course could be found. This was one of the streams that fed the Cwtsh-y-Cym.

The house had various occupants, most of whom had maritime connections. In 1851 it was the home of H H Parry, a retired Shipping Agent. Other residents included John Batchelor and the ship owner Valentine Trayes. W A Plisson, a French-born owner of the Plisson Steam Navigtion Company of Mountstuart Square, who is reputed to have built the sea wall, lived there between 1910 and 1920. He was followed by Howard Neale of Neale and West Trawlers fame.

During the Second World War the house and grounds were commandeered by the American Forces. After the war ended the house deteriorated and was eventually demolished.

NORTH PIER

The entrance to Penarth Dock was originally protected by two massive wooden greenheart piers known as the North and South Piers. Both were demolished to make way for the Marina development.

OAKLEIGH TERRACE

A grand terrace of Victorian town houses that run from the Police Station to the lane behind Holy Nativity Church. Plaques high on the wall of the house at the entrance to Windsor Lane commemorate the name. In the 1890s the terrace became part of Windsor Road. The name is possibly a corruption of Oakly (see below).

OAKLY PARK

The park at Oakly, near Bromfield, was once a Royal forest to which Sir William Herbert was appointed Keeper during the reign of Henry VIII. The present house was originally the Keeper's Lodge, but was enlarged at various times until the final additions were made in 1840 by the Honourable Robert Henry Clive.

The estate was in the hands of the Herbert family until it was purchased from Henry, Earl of Powis, by Robert, Lord Clive of Plassey. There is also an Oakly Place close to Broomfield Street in Grangetown, Cardiff.

ONE, TWO, THREE WOODS

This pleasant wood, now sadly thinned and vandalised, bisects the large council housing estate built behind Redlands Road. The wood itself is cut through by a stream that originally ran from two ponds - one that lay just behind Ivy Cottage, and the other where today's Ivy Street and Machen Street back on to each other. The ponds were both filled in to allow for urbanization, although thedried out water course of part of the stream can still be seen at the northern edge of the Victoria Playing Field, while a stream still runs through the wood down to Sully. The derivation of the name One, Two, Three Woods is not known.

In 1890 farmer Rees of Cornerswell Farm was instructed by the Local Board to keep the stream in the One, Two, Three Woods clear of detritus and brambles.[110]

ORCHARD LEDGES

Cardiff's Alexandra Dock, which was opened in 1907, was built on land reclaimed from the sea by tipping slag and spoil onto the Orchard Ledges, an extensive area of mud and shingle that dried out at low water. Local legend has it that the ledges were a petrified forest. Paterson suggests the name is derived from the Old Norse orfjara which translates as a reef uncovered, or a bank uncovered at low tide[111].

PADDLING POOL

This was a shallow oblong concrete pool that was covered at high water and then retained sea water as the tide ebbed. The pool was sited roughly halfway between Penarth Pier and the Dardanelles sewer outlet slipway, approximately at the point where the slipway that runs beneath the multi-storey car park is to be found today. The pool was much loved by the children of the town. Indeed,

[110]   Penarth Observer, 1890.
[111]   Paterson, ibid.

the author had his first taste of salt water from being allowed to crawl around
in the pool as a small infant!

PATCH

As with the Orchard Ledges, the Patch was a large bank of mud and shingle
that dried out at low water, although it was not as extensive as the Ledges. The
Patch and the Cefn-y-Wrach separated the mouth of the River Taff from the
mouth of the River Ely in the near vicinity of Penarth Head. A navigational
hazard to shipping, the Patch was dredged away when the Penarth Dock was
built in 1859.

PAGET PLACE

This charming row of substantial Victorian villas in a quiet, tree-lined
backwater of Penarth was shown as Plymouth Place on the 1859 town plan. It
then became Plymouth Road North before changing its name yet again to
Paget Place, the name by which it has been known from around 1886 onwards.
The Earl of Plymouth, Robert George Windsor Clive, married Alberta Paget in
1883. During its existence as Plymouth Road North the residents included
George Pile, a boat-builder who lived at no. 1, Mr Richard Davies, Deputy
Dock Master who lived at Wave Villa, and a person going by the splendid name
of Gabriel de Boisduval who lived at no. 10.

PAGET ROAD

Paget Road stretches from Queen's Road to Paget Terrace and until the time
of the Second World War it was part of Dock Road. It used to have beautiful
wrought iron balconies at first floor level running along the whole terrace, all
now sadly removed.

PAGET TERRACE

As with Paget Road, the Terrace was part of Dock Road until the 1880s, when
its name was changed.

PEMBROKE TERRACE

In 1859 Church Lane (now Coronation Terrace) stretched up as far as the north
side of St. Augustine's Church. When the houses were built at the top of

Church Lane - many of them in distinctive local yellow brick - they were named Church PlaceNorth. By the 1890s they were included as part of Lord Street, before becoming Pembroke Terrace.

In 1704 Charlotte Herbert had married Thomas, Viscount Windsor. She was a direct descendent of William Herbert, First Earl of Pembroke, who died in 1570. Charlotte's father was Philip, Seventh Earl of Pembroke, who died in 1683.

PENARTH

Documentary evidence on early Penarth is less than satisfactory, especially when compared with other parishes in the area. The earliest records are ecclesiastical and date from the 12th century. In 1148 a priory was founded in Bristol by the Augustine Canons, who were also known as the Austin Canons and the Black Canons. Norman landholders, who had only recently arrived on both sides of the Severn Sea, gifted large tracts of land to the Canons.

In 1151 Gilbert de Constantin (see Cosmeston) gave land lying between the rivers Ely and Taff to the Canons. At about the same time Osbert of Penarth gifted the Order most of the land now known as Penarth, while John de Cogan gifted them a further 22 acres of land near Penarth. From the records that were kept detailing these gifts we know that the Prior of the newly-built Priory of St. Augustine's had also become Lord of the Manor of Penarth. The Parish church for the town was built on Penarth Head between 1186-1191 when the Lord of the Manor was the Prior of Bristol and Bishop of Llandaff, William Saltmarsh.

G O Pierce[112] lists many spellings for Penarth, including Penharth (1266), Pennarth (13th century), Pennart (again in the 13th century), Penarthe and Pennarthe (the 1550s), Pennarth (1600) and Penurth (1695), and there are many more. There are numerous theories surrounding the derivation of the name, the most likely being that of the Welsh word 'garth' meaning a promontory, ridge or height, and another Welsh word 'pen', meaning a head or hill.

PENARTH BRICKWORKS

The site of the Penarth Brickworks can still be seen. A massive quarry dug out from the escarpment that used to be covered by Adam's Wood, the area is now a housing estate, Cogan Garden Village.

[112]   G O Pierce, ibid.

The Brickworks opened in about 1880. Its first manager was Jeremiah Pickersgill. The Works were generally referred to as the Marl Pit - something of an understatement for the massive hole dug out of the escarpment.

When the Works were at their peak a number of large kilnswere kept busy. There was a tall brick chimney, a large reservoir on a plateau in the north-eastern corner of the quarry, and an extensive complex of tramways laid out in a three-pronged formation. The only reminders of this once busy brickworks are the high sides of the quarry and a section of the original boundary wall. Ironically this was built of stone and not brick.

PENARTH COLLEGIATE SCHOOL

This was yet another of the town's many private schools and operated in the late 19th, early 20th centuries from numbers 7 and 8 Albert Crescent. At the turn of the century, when the school was at its busiest, the two Principals, Mr and Mrs Apel, employed a large staff including a Headmaster, Mr J. S Grant (M.A. Jesus College, Oxford), a violin teacher, Mr Paul Draper, and a Drill Master, Sgt. Major Matthews.

PENARTH DOCK (ALMOST LOST)

The Penarth Harbour Dock and Railway Act was passed on 27 July 1857 and work on building the dock commenced in 1859. The dock was opened (albeit it had not been fully completed[113]) on Saturday, 10 June 1965. The William Cory was the first vessel to enter the Dock.

The basin was 400 ft long and the dock itself 2,100 ft. The basin was 330 ft wide and the dock 370 ft wide. There were ten coaling tips in the dock and two in the basin. Two of these tips came from the Ely Tidal Harbour.

Following an Act of Parliament passed in 1881 the Penarth Dock was extended westwards. The extension was officially opened on 9 April 1884 and meant the dock was now 2,900 ft long. The deep water area for the entire dock complex was as follows: Penarth Dock 23 acres; Penarth Basin 3.5 acres; the Penarth Tidal Harbour 55 acres. There were 14 coal tips, served by the High Level Sidings on the south side of the dock, two moveable tips on the north side, and four moveable tips on the north side of the basin. (Two tips on the

---

[113]   Mountford & Sprinks, ibid.

southern side of the basin were only short-lived). In addition there were a five further tips in the Tidal Harbour in 1884. In 1878 there had been 11.[114]

PENARTH FLATS

A term widely used up until the building of Penarth Dock to describe the vast expanse of mud between Penarth and the River Taff. It is only rarely heard today.

PENARTH GRAMMAR SCHOOL (LOST)

This school was opened in about 1880 by the Reverend John D. Edwards and Mr Sidney Gibson at Ebenezer House, West House Road. The house later became 14 Westbourne Road when the road was renamed in about 1890. In 1896 the school was taken over by Miss Ferris, who continued to operate a school at 14 Westbourne Road until 1902 when she moved to 13 Stanwell Road.

PENARTH HARBOUR

This rather misleading title has been used to describe the extensive area of mud flats between Penarth and Cardiff from the earliest days of maritime endeavours on the Severn Sea. As recently as 1878 W P Williams[115] wrote: "Penarth is four miles south-west from Cardiff by land, and about two by water, from which the town is severed by the estuary formed by the junction of two rivers, the Taff and the Ely. A third river which flows east of Cardiff [the Rhymney River] joins its sister streams in forming Penarth Harbour." B H Malkin noted: "Penarth Harbour is the best and safest in the Bristol Channel"[116].

Since the earliest times of Man sailing the Severn Sea, Penarth Harbour, with its safe holding mud for anchoring and the protection given by Penarth Head and the Ridge, was an ideal place to dodge the tides and the prevailing south-west winds. A Cardiff Directory for 1796 stated "Three miles below the Town of Cardiff is the harbour called Pennarth and it is very commodious for

[114] Mountford & Sprinks, ibid.
[115] W. P. Williams: Windsor Monograph. 1878. Ibid.
[116] Ibid.

ships and vessels detained in the Bristol Channel by westerly winds."[117] Although called a harbour, there were never any of the features usually associated with harbours per se such as Minehead and Watchet for instance such as harbour walls, quays, warehouses and so on.

On 24 August 1793 a vessel that had been due to anchor in Penarth Harbour put into Barry Harbour instead, the crew having been tipped off in the Channel by a passing ship that there was a Press Gang waiting at Penarth. To prevent their being pressed, they forced the Captain to land them at Barry, from where they started to walk towards Cardiff.[118] "At about 3 pm, seamen armed with cutlasses, bludgeons etc. passed through Cardiff. They had landed at Barry to prevent being pressed at Pennarthe. A quarter of an hour later a press gang of 14 men, well-armed came in pursuit".[119] The Press Gang caught up with the seamen at Rumney. A large crowd of locals surrounded the Press Gang anddeclared their support for the seamen. After a skirmish the Press Gang retired and the local people took the ship's crew to a local hostelry to calm their nerves.

PENARTH HEAD INN

This large, well-constructed inn with its adjoining stables, lofts and outhouses, was built in roughly the 1730s by Edward Edwards, an acknowledged smuggler of long standing. In 1738 the Customs at Penarth seized tobacco and spirits from a small coastal vessel. The goods were intended for "a man of substance named Edwards, who lately had built a house by the harbour where there never was one before ..... he is an old offender and is reputed to have built large cellars to store his goods"[120]. The King's boat, the Customs vessel, was moored at the nearby Cwtch-y-Cwm and Edwards continually threatened to cut its moorings and to attack the officers.

The Inn was built right up against the cliff face at the top of an extensive sloping but sheltered shingle beach. In 1750 the Customs Surveyor, William Richards, asked the Revenue Commissioners to buy the Penarth Head Inn "near where the King's boat is moored". He cited a lengthy list of reasons why they should give consideration to this recommendation, including the fact that

[117] B. A. Malkin: The Scenery, Antiquities and Biography of South Wales.
[118] J. Bird (publisher): Complete Directory and Guide to Cardiff. 1796.
[119] J. Bird: Diaries 1790-1807. Edited by H. M. Thomas. 1987.
[120] Ibid.

Penarth Head Inn built c.1730's, demolished 1864.

"It [would] prevent the smuggler from living there -it will keep the masts and saylls dry ... protect the poor officers from the inclemency of the weather"[121].

By the 1800s the Inn had put its nefarious beginnings behind it and had become a popular watering hole for the crews of vessels anchored on the mud of Penarth Harbour, Penarth Flats and Penarth Roads. Paying guests were also catered for. The Census of 1841 shows the landlord to have been W Williams who lived there with his wife and son, three servants and four visitors. The son was classed as a grocer and the visitors were Morgan Lisle, an iron master, his wife and their two sons. In the 1851 Census we find W. Richards and his wife still running the Inn but by now there were only two servants and just one visitor in residence. The 1861 Census shows W. Jones (widower) as landlord, with one servant and three visitors. The Inn was demolished in 1864 to make way for the Customs Building.

PENARTH HOTEL (see also Gibbs' Home and Headlands)

The Penarth Hotel was built by the Taff Vale Railway in the 1860s and opened in 1868[122] in anticipation of business from shipowners, shipping agents, ships' captains and so on. These expectations, unfortunately, were never fulfilled.

In a bid to attract visitors it was planned to bring a passenger line from Cogan to a station to be built at the bottom of Dock Beach Hill at the easternmost extremity of the High Level Sidings, although this idea was soon dropped.

The hotel was never a commercial success and the lease was taken over by a Mr W G Jones in 1873 and then by Mr Wain of the Cardiff Royal Hotel in 1879. The Census of 1871 shows that the hotel manager at that time was T. Leyshon. Also in residence were Mrs Leyshon, their four daughters and two sons, plus two members of staff. There was just one paying guest recorded. The Census also showed that the accommodation in the stable block was occupied by W Dimond, his wife and son, and Mr Dimond's brother. Ten years later the 1881 Census returns show thirteen people in residence, five of whom were paying guests, the other eight being members of staff. A ship owner, Robert Glaister Sharpe, aged 60, from the then busy port of Maryport, Cumbria was one of the guests.

---

[121] Chappell, ibid.
[122] P. Carradice: Headlands School. 1991.

117

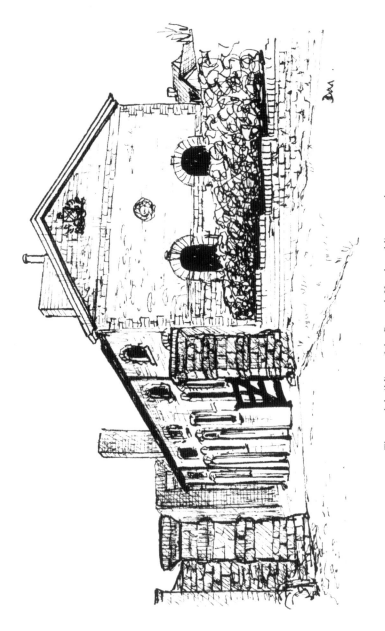

The south building of the Penarth Hotel, stabling complex.

Happily, this imposing Victorian building is still standing and indeed remains largely unspoiled, as does the beautiful and extensive complex comprising stabling block, coach houses and stable staff accommodation that was built alongside. Hilling suggests the hotel was "... basically classical in conception -a row of palladian type pedimented windows on the first floor"[123].

In 1873 when the hotel was taken over by Mr W G Jones, he placed an advert in the local press which read: "W G Jones begs to acquaint the nobility, gentry, clergy and his numerous friends who kindly patronized him at the Scudmore Arms, Pontrilas, Herefordshire, that he had taken the above first-class hotel ... the rooms are all light and airy ... the Coffee Room being the handsomest in South Wales ... Good stabling and coach houses. Billiard, Croquet and Archery Grounds[124]."

PENARTH HOUSE

In 1888 Philip Morel with his wife Martha and their four children were living at 14 Park Place, Cardiff. They then moved to 40 Park Place before moving again to Lavernock House, now the Golden Hind (see St. Mary's Well Bay). By 1892 the family had taken up resident in Penarth House, which he "built for himself"[125].

This massive red brick house, all gables, bays and a tower -possibly Penarth's largest and grandest house - was built at the southern end of Marine Parade in four acres of beautifully laidout grounds, the whole surrounded by a massive brick boundary wall. The reception rooms were magnificent, the drawing room was furnished in the style of Louis XV[126]. The servants lived on the third floor.

The house was demolished and the site is now a small housing estate and home to Morel Court, which was built in the grounds. All that remains is the beautiful mellow brick boundary wall and the many elegant original gateways into the grounds.

On 2 December 1892, the Local Board agreed "to erect a Bray's Burner (gas lamp) in the centre of the square opposite Mr Morel's mansion[127].

[123] Hilling, ibid.
[124] Cardiff Directory, 1873.
[125] Gibbs, ibid.
[126] Gibbs, ibid.
[127] Local Board Minutes for 1892. Penarth Library.

PENARTH LODGE SCHOOL

This private school for boys was built in the early 1880s and was classified as being in Westbourne Road. Later, when Archer Road was built in the 1890s, the Lodge became part of Archer Road. The Proprietor and Headmaster was Mr H. Field M.A. The charming red-brick building is unusual in design and is now a private residence.

PENARTH MEWS (LOST)

Solomon Andrews, the archetypal Samuel Smiles hero and quintessential Victorian entrepreneur, built a large business complex in Glebe Street and Ludlow Lane in the 1870s, centred around the Penarth Mews. The complex stretched from what is today Rowleys, the Jewellers, down to Albert Road in one direction and down Glebe Street in the other as far as the St Fagan's Castle Inn. It included stables, coach houses, a large yard and Andrews's Small Hall with its shops, coffee tavern and ticket offices. Andrews ran a horse-drawn bus service to Cardiff from Glebe Street, as well as hansom cabs, a bakers, a funeral parlour, a travel service and a furniture moving business. A large portion of the original Penarth Mews site is now occupied by the Royal Mail building and car park.

PENARTH PIER HEAD TAP - See Marine Hotel

PENARTH PONTOON

In 1909 a floating dock, a pontoon dry dock, was built at Westminster, London and towed to Penarth Roads. It arrived in October 1909, whereupon the pontoon was divided into two sections before being towed to the western end of the Dock (the new extension) where it was re-assembled.

The pontoon was 382 feet long and 75 feet wide and had been built by Swan, Hunter, Wigham, Richardson Limited of Wallsend-on-Tyne at their Westminster yard. The first vessel to use the floating dry-dock was a three masted barquentine, The Baltzig of Riga.

The pontoon worked on a very simple principle. Water was pumped into the sections whereupon it submerged. The vessel to be repaired was towed into position above the pontoon, the water was pumped out again causing the pontoon to rise to the surface, leaving the vessel high and dry.

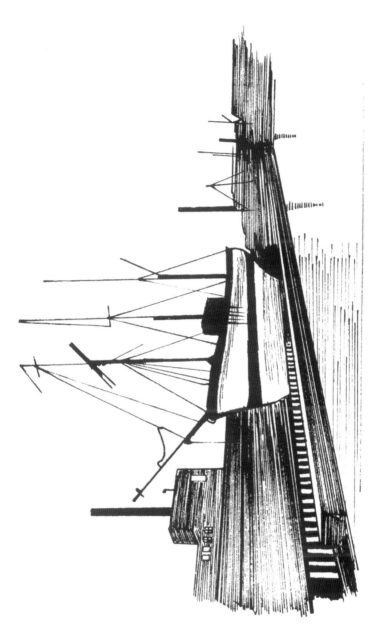

The three mast barquentine 'The Baltzig of Piga', 1909.

When Penarth Dock finally closed in 1963, the pontoon was partially scrapped, then submerged before being covered with a municipal rubbish tip.

PENARTH RAILWAY HOTEL

This isolated public house stands on land reclaimed from the mud of the Penarth Flats (see Grass and Mud Points). For years the pub was known as the Red House, a name that was certainly in use during the period 1914-1923 when Daniel Davies was the landlord. Its derivation remains a mystery.

The first landlord of the Penarth Railway Hotel was R C Heard in 1871. An early Police Report gives us a clear description of the pub and shows that the house consisted of "Accommodation including bedrooms, exclusive of those for family and staff, a basement with two cellars and a kitchen, on the ground floor a bar 11 feet by 6 feet 3 inches, a Tap Room 20 feet 4 inches by 11 feet 4 inches, and a Smoke Room 23 feet by 12.5 feet, without a small yard with stabling for four horses. On the first floor four bedrooms for staff."

For many years the pub was frequented by the crews of sailing vessels, ketches and schooners that were calling into the Ely Tidal Harbour for coal right up until the late 1950s.

In May 1847 at Cardiff, the master of the vessel Catherine, sailing out of Clonkelly, was charged with "... illegally landing 25 Irish persons, women and children, onto the mud flats from open boats at the point where the Red House stands today, this contrary to the Passengers Act of 1842.[128]" The captain was fined £200 and given two months in prison. His defence for landing the immigrants on the isolated mud flats was "fear of getting abused by the inhabitants of Cardiff ... because the Irish people were in such a diseased and destitute state".

PENARTH ROADS

The Roads can be said to cover the area from Lavernock Point to Penarth Head and out to the sandbanks. The Roads and Penarth Harbour afforded the only safe haven and anchorage from south-westerly gales in the Bristol Channel.

Vessels were protected in the Roads from the prevailing winds by the cliffs of Penarth Plateau, Head and Ridge, while the sea bed - a mixture of "mud,

---

[128]   G. Smith: Smuggling in the Bristol Channel, 1700-1850. 1989.

marl and shingle gave a good holding ground"[129]. Maritime records, especially in the days of sail, but even later under steam power, record vessels leaving Cardiff, Barry, Penarth, Swansea etc. and sailing out into the Atlantic for as far as 300, 400 or even 500 miles before being driven back by extremely bad weather and seeking refuge in the Penarth Roads.

The redoubtable Captain Wallace, master of the Cutty Sark left Penarth with a cargo of coal bound for the America Pacific Fleet. The vessel had barely started down the Bristol Channel when she was compelled to return and anchor in Penarth Roads while "a wild south-west gale shrieked up the Bristol Channel for three days of flying scud, raging seas and howling wind![130]"

Trounce relates: "I can remember seeing 200 to 300 vessels in the Roads ..... I have known vessels lying there wind bound for between 2 to 3 months, especially in the winter with strong westerly and south westerly gales."

He also relates how "A fine American clipper, the Charlotte A Stanley, lay in Penarth Roads for 24 days ... too big to enter the West Dock and awaited the opening of the new East Dock 20/6/1855". At about the same time "..... a mutiny on the American vessel the African anchored in Penarth Roads - several crewmen injured and one James Harley died of his injuries in the Cardiff Infirmary"[131].

PENARTH SQUARE (LOST)

This was another colloquial name for Albert Square. Mr Rowland informs us that Penarth Square and the area now known as Alexandra Gardens were used for communal grazing right up until landscaping took place in the 1890s. The use of the Square for grazing and fairs (see Albert Square) caused much public disquiet and brought letters of complaint to the press and the Local Board. On 23 September 1892 a letter to the local press complained that "... an unmitigated nuisance now exists in Penarth Square. This classic ground, close to the spot Einion ap-Collwyn and his ally Robert Fitzhamon stood - someone has let this piece of ground for a horrid whirl around affair with a horrid, horrid screech attached - it was bad enough before -donkeys which made night hideous with their vesper hymns -closeto the Assembly Hall of the local

---

[129] Captain White: Admiralty Survey, 1823-7.
[130] Basil Lubbock: The Log of the Cutty Sark. 1949.
[131] Trounce, ibid.

dignitaries, close to the Education Department and close to colleges and seminaries galore"[132].

PENARTH MOORS (LOST)

Cardiff's former massive municipal refuse dump in Ferry Road to covers what had been an area of flooding tide fields known as Penarth Moors. Earlier names included Pennardismore, Pennard's Moor and the Saltmarsh.

PENARTH TUTORIAL COLLEGE

The very large town houses that were originally numbered one and two Stanwell Road were built in the early 1880s. Number 1 was occupied by Alfred Holman, a ship broker, ship owner and director of Fry, Holmon, Fry of 113 Bute Street, Cardiff. Number 2, meanwhile, was occupied by a Mr John Thomas. By 1900 the houses had been renumbered 9 and 10 Stanwell Road and were occupied by Charles Aitken MD and R. F. Nell M.R.C.S respectively. By 1892 the houses had been renumbered yet again to become 18 and 19 Stanwell Road and were occupied by Arthur Leach (no. 18) and Henry Radcliffe, a ship owner (no. 19).

The Tutorial College had been opened at 2 Albert Crescent during the 1880s by Mr Jones, but was demolished in 1905 whereupon Mr Jones moved the establishment to 9 and 10 Stanwell Road. In 1910 the College was taken over by Mr Thomas Wynn and later moved to Westwood House where it became known as Westwood College. The building is now the Penarth Conservative Club.

During the First World War the buildings were used as a Military Hospital from 1917 to 1919. In 1922 No. 9 Stanwell Road was occupied by Mr Oliver Wilmore and later that same year it became the Washington Hotel, which was opened by Captain W H Bevan.

PENUAL

This small Welsh Baptist Chapel was originally two houses in Plassey Street which were converted into a place of worship in 1877. The conversion work was carried out by Mr D G Price, founder of Price Brothers. There were two

[132] Penarth Observer, 1892.

small cottages at the rear of the property, both of which remained in occupation until the 1960s.

The Salvation Army took over the chapel and it was only recently demolished to make way for a handsome new Citadel on the site. The Salvation Army first came to the town in 1884.[133]

PENTWYN FARM (LOST)

The existence of this farm, one of the many small farms that existed in the Parish of Penarth before urbanization, can be traced back to as long ago as 1700. G O Pierce translates Twyn as a hill, hillock, tump, knoll, or rising ground, while pen is the Welsh word for a head or height[134]. This would tend to point to a location in the northern part of the parish. In the Glamorgan Land Tax Assessment of 1784, it is stated that "... the Glebelands in Penarth were owned by the Rev. George Richards, Rector of Penarth, the lands being farmed by William and Rosser Thomas." The two farms worked by the Thomas brothers were both on Glebeland, and thus lay to the north of the Parish, and could perhaps have been the Norden and Pentwyn Farms.

PHILLIPS' FARM (LOST)

As in the case of Pentwyn, the location of this farm is not known. It appears on records as long ago as 1700. However, the Tax Assessment of 1786 shows that a William Hunt owned Cornerswell Farm and that this was leased to and farmed by John Phillips. Perhaps Cornerswell Farm was also known as Phillips' Farm.

PENARTH SLIPWAY (LOST)

The Penarth Ship Building and Repairing Company Limited built the Penarth Slipway in 1879 under the aegis of James Edwards, the Dock Superintendent of the Taff Vale Railway. James Edwards had built and lived in the house known as Westwood in Stanwell Road (now the Penarth Conservative Club). A section of the slipway and some of the jetties can still be seen on the southern bank of the River Ely, but will soon be lost when the Cardiff Barrage is built.

[133]   R. Thorne, ibid.
[134]   G O Pierce, ibid.

The slipway was advertised as being 867 feet long and capable of taking vessels of up to 300 feet and 2,200 tons gross register. They could undertake extensive repairs and also lengthen ships. The usual method for wooden or iron vessels was for the vessel to be cut in half, the two sections pulled apart and a new middle section put into place. An early advertisement claimed that "Vessels could be placed at the top of the slipway, where work is not interfered with through the taking up of other vessels"[135]. The Slipway and its yard were also served by blacksmiths, boilermakers, coppersmiths, plumbers, shipwrights, tinsmiths, etc. and had its own private railway sidings running from the dockside into the yard and to the top of the slipway.

Shipbuilding was also undertaken and the vessels produced included the County of Lancaster built in 1884, 214 grossregistered tonnage, which was a tramp steamer. It sank in 1911. Another tramp steamer was the Aira Force built in 1891. 145 feet long, the vessel was later renamed the Seaforth but it too sank, in 1929. Another vessel built at the Slipway was the Iona, a double-ended paddle steamer of 64 gross registered tonnage, 91 feet long and 18 feet wide built for the Cardiff Penarth Ferry Company in 1883. It was owned by a prominent Penarth shipowner, Mr H. J Vellacott. The vessel was sold to Mr Tom Morel in 1896 and owned by him until 1903. It was finally broken up for scrap in 1913[136].

In 1897 a model of a proposed new steam vessel for use by the Mission to Seamen and called the Eirene (Peace) was put on view at the Cardiff Coal Exchange. The boat, designed by Mr Monroe of Penarth (an ancestor of Cllr. Anthony Ernest), manager of the Slipway, was already in course of construction at the yard belonging to the Penarth Shipbuilding Company as a replacement for the old sailing vessel also named the Eirene. The new ship was to be 80 ft long, 70 tons register, and would be fitted with 125 HP engines. Under the ministry of the Rev. C. W. H. Browne, MA the vessel would serve the area from Newport to Lundy.

PICTUREDROME (LOST)

Solomon Andrews's Large Hall in Albert Road, built in 1892, went under numerous guises during its varied career. In 1911 it was called the Picturedrome and it was one of the first cinemas in the town. At that time it was

[135]   Cardiff Directory, 1885.
[136]   G. Farr: West Country Passenger Steamers. 1967.

managed by Mr R H Thomas, who was paid a salary of 30 shillings a week. By 1924 it had become the Albert Hall Cinema when it was run by the ubiquitous Willmore Brothers, who leased the hall from the Andrews family.

PIER PAVILION

Penarth Pier had two pavilions. The first was the Penarth Pier Bijou Pavilion - a large wooden building built at the seaward end of the Pier in 1907, and which burned down on 3 August 1931. The other pavilion was the new Pier Pavilion, which opened on 18 May 1929. In 1932 it was run as the short-lived Penarth Pavilion Cinema until a short while later it became the Marina Ballroom in 1934.

PLASSEY STREET

This is yet another street name commemorating Robert Clive, Clive of India. Plassey, a town in Bengal, India, was one of Clive's most famous victories in which he avenged the terrible atrocities of the Black Hole of Calcutta by defeating the perpetrator, the Surajah Dowlah, Nabob of Bengal. Clive's unparalleled victory at the fearful Battle of Plassey took place on 23 June 1757. With only 3,000 men, he defeated and routed the Surajah Dowlah and his force of 70,000 troops. The Surajah was captured and executed. Clive was elevated to the Peerage, taking the title Lord Robert Clive, Baron Plassey, on 17 March 1762. He became a Knight of the Grand Order of the Bath in 1764. Clive died ten years later in 1774 at the early age of 48.

PLYMOUTH ROAD

Thomas Hickman, son of Elizabeth, co-heiress to the Baron Windsor, and her husband Dixey Hickman of Kew, became the Earl of Plymouth on 6 December 1682. By his first wife, Ann, daughter of Sir William Saville, Bart., he had one son, Other Windsor, who was born on 12 September 1659. His second wife, Ursula, daughter of Sir Thomas Widdington, bore him two sons, the eldest being Viscount Windsor and the younger Baron Mountjoy. Thomas Hickman, Earl of Plymouth, died on 10 November 1687.

Plymouth Road is one of the town's most charming thoroughfares, a long and wide, tree-lined road of substantial stone-built Victorian town houses. It

© Diane Mead

The Penarth Pier with the 'New' Pavilion at the landward end, later re-named the 'Marina' and then the 'Commodore'.

has had many distinguished residents, including the composer, Dr Joseph Parry, who lived with his family at no. 23 during the 1890s, and the brewer, S.A. Brain, who lived at Roxburgh.

POLICE STATION

The Police Station in Windsor Road, a fine Victorian building in local stone, was built in 1865 and has always been in the charge of an Inspector[137]. Viewed from Windsor Road, the building has three sections to it - the Magistrates Court to the right, the Inspector's living quarters in the middle, and the Police Offices to the left, with the Constables' living accommodation above. This has changed over the years. The Court has been closed, and all the Police Officers now live off station.

The Census of 1871 shows that Inspector Adams, his wife, four daughters and a son were living in the Police House, and that four constables (Pickwick, Williams, Llewellyn and Brace) were in residence in the Station's accommodation[138].

The 1881 Census shows that an Inspector Tom King, his wife and six children were living in the Police House, while three unmarried Constables were using the accommodation wing - Messrs. Berry, Evans and Llewellyn. The cells, meanwhile, had just one prisoner in them, John Anstee, a mariner from Bridgwater, Somerset.

During the period 1884 - 1902 the town's Fire Engine was based at the Police Station. The horses used to draw it were brought from Solomon Andrews's Penarth Mews in Ludlow Lane.

POWELL'S LANE (LOST)

Shown on a map of Penarth produced in early 1859 as Powell's Lane, this thoroughfare is now known by the rather more apt name of Steep Street. The derivation of the original name is uncertain, although Thomas Powell, of Powell Duffryn fame, was a director of the original Dock Company (as were Crawshay Bailey, John Batchelor, W. F. Cartwright, Lewis David, Henry James Evans, James Insole, John Mason and George H.W. Windsor-Clive).

[137] R. Thorne, ibid.
[138] E. A. Benjamin: Penarth, 1841-1871. 1980.

POWIS ROAD

Robert Clive, Baron Plassey, using the wealth he acquired in India, bought lands from the Earl of Powis. Clive's son, Edward, married Henrietta Antonia, daughter of Henry Arthur Herbert, the Earl of Powis in 1784. On his father's death, Edward became the second Lord Clive, Baron Clive, Baron Powis and Viscount Clive, all listed in the English Peerage. He was later created Earl of Powis. His second son was Robert Henry Clive who married the Baroness Windsor.

PRIMROSE LANE (LOST)

This was an early and colloquial name for the lane that runs from Lavernock Road, past the old Lavernock Station, and down to St. Mary's Well Bay.

The local press reported that on the afternoon of Wednesday, 15 June 1892, the Windsor Road Congregationalists marched from their Windsor Road Iron Church to the town's railway station[139], from whence they travelled by train to Lavernock Station. This had opened on 1 December 1887 as Lavernock Halt, and closed on 6 May 1968, a victim of Beeching's Axe. From here they made their way via Primrose Lane to the beach where they skipped, played on swings, had games of cricket and rounders, ran races and enjoyed the refreshments provided before returning home by train, arriving back at Penarth at 8 p.m.

PRINCE OF WALES THEATRE (LOST)

As with the Lyceum Theatre, the Prince of Wales Theatre does not, strangely enough, appear in any of the published histories of Penarth, nor in any early guide books or street directories. The only references that have been traced were included in a short report contained in the 9 March 1901 issue of the Penarth Observer which noted: "Mr John Johnstone has applied for a three month temporary licence for the Prince of Wales." The Penarth Urban District Council Minutes for Monday, 4 March 1901, confirm that "Mr John Johnstone of 8 High Street has applied for a temporary licence for the Prince of Wales in High Street."

The exact location of the theatre is as yet unknown. However, by 1901 High Street was already almost completely built up. The theatre could well have

---

[139] Penarth Observer, 1892.

been in the Drill Hall of the former Artillery Quarters, possibly converted for use as a theatre. This was located where 31 to 36 High Street stand today.

PROSPECT HOUSE (LOST)

This name causes a great deal of confusion. It appears to have been used colloquially and for only short periods in relation to Cliff Villa, Northcliff and Uppercliff. The fact that the name was used for two houses may have been due to the fact that John Batchelor lived in both and had built a tower (later demolished on the orders of the Windsor-Clive family) at Cliff Villa, Northcliff, in order presumably to enjoy the 'prospect'.

QUARRIES

Quarrying in Penarth had certainly been taking place as long ago as the Roman occupation and it continued right up until the middle of this century. In the early 1802 large quantities of stone were quarried at Penarth and shipped to Newport where it was used to construct sea walls at the mouth of the River Usk[140].

During the 19th century there were numerous quarries in the parish. A very large deep one was sited to the front of what is today's Harbour View Road, and there were a number of smaller satellite quarries. One was located on the slope in front of High View Road, and another could be found at the end of the path that leads west from High View Road to the western extremity of Penarth Ridge. Until recently the remains of a kiln could be seen to the right of the path that runs westward. If it is still there, it is now hidden by thick undergrowth. A further two small quarries also existed - one in front of what is now Paget Road, and another opposite the houses in Paget Terrace. They were linked by a complex system of tramways that ran down to the Williams Sidings, just off the High Level Sidings. This area is now in part covered by the Billybanks flats.

A small quarry was worked at the corner of Pembroke Terrace and Albert Road, and Belle Vue Park was a limestone quarry. The log book for the Penarth Board School in Albert Road records that on 16th March 1877 "Two small boys drowned in the quarry opposite the school"[141].

---

[140]   J. W. Dawson: Commerce and Customs. 1932.
[141]   School Log.

There was another quarry at the point where Jubilee Lane meets Church Avenue. Falconhurst in Bradford Place and its extensive, well kept gardens stand on the site of a 19th centuryquarry.

The area around St. Peters Avenue was another quarry, as was the site of the club house and pitches belonging to the Old Penarthians' Rugby Club. Finally, there were large quarries on both sides of Lavernock Road, which used to belong to the Lower Penarth Cement Works (South Wales Portland Cement and Limeworks). The quarries to the east of Lavernock Road have been filled in, as have part of the quarries to the west. The rest have been flooded and now make up the Cosmeston Lakes.

QUEEN'S BENCH (lost)

The town's first Methodist Chapel was built in Arcot Street in 1863/64, and it later became the Anglican church of St Pauls. It is now the home of the Penarth Boxing Club. Before acquiring the Methodist Chapel, the Anglicans worshipped in an iron church (see Church Terrace) that had been built in 1881[142] on an extensive grassy bank or hillock known as the Queen's Bench. The derivation is as yet unknown, although it is interesting to note that the houses built on the site after the church was demolished in 1906, as well as later houses built in 1909, are now in Queen's Road.

RANNY BAY AND RANNY POINT

Paterson suggest the derivation in from the old Norse word rani or hog's snout[143] Certainly the promontory when seen from the sea as the Vikings would have seen it as they swept up the Bristol Channel might well have resembled a hog's snout. The Vikings had a penchant for applying animal names to natural features such as hills, promontories, cliffs etc.

RAITHWAITE (see Cwrt-y-Vil)

This imposing mansion was built for Lascelles Carr in the 1870s when it was originally known as Cwrt-y-Vil House. The Pymen family bought it in the early part of the 20th century, moving into the house from Marine Parade and changing its name to Raithwaite in the process.

---

[142] This date of 1881 needs further research. 1892 would appear to be more accurate.
[143] Paterson, ibid.

RANDELL'S FARM (lost)

This farm stood roughly where Lansdowne House stands today. The 1841 Census shows the farm as being occupied by William Randell who was born in 1800 in Somerset. He had married Ann Phillips (perhaps from Phillips' Farm) on 16 August 1834. They had six children - Mary born 1836, Ann 1838, William 1839, Thomas 1841, John 1843 and Margaret 1848.

Margaret married Evan Thomas Morse on 3 October 1873. Her new husband lived at 26 Salop Street and was a Bristol Channel pilot, as was his father, David Morse. On 20 November 1872, her sister Mary married Thomas Griffiths, the landlord of the Albion Hotel in Glebe Street. His father, John Griffiths, was also an Innkeeper, although the location of the premises he ran is not known. Randell's Farm was demolished around about the 1880s.

REDLANDS (lost)

This magnificent house was built for J. Pyke Thompson in the early 1880s and must have vied with Dros-y-Mor and Penarth House for the honour of being the town's largest and finest house - all now lost. Redlands was built on land that had previously been part of Randell's Farm. Thompson resided at Redlands until 1895 when the house was taken over by Eustace Clothier, who lived there until 1899 when it was sold to the brewer, S.A.Brain, who changed its name to Roxburgh. Brain lived there until 1910, when Thomas Morel moved in. The house was the Morel family home until is was vacated, demolished and the houses that make up Roxburgh Court built. All that remains is the very impressive red-brick boundary wall and Turner House, which was built in1888.

RED HOUSE (see Penarth Railway Hotel)

This public house has had many landlords since it was opened in 1871. Its first was R. C. Head, then in the 1880s and 1890s it was run by J. F. Deslandes and subsequently E. Deslandes. It was in the hands of the Young family for nearly half a century between 1933 and 1981.

Perhaps its most notable landlord was Andrew Garrick who ran the premises during the 1890s. He was also a Master Mariner on sailing ships and had a house in Windsor Road, Cogan. Captain Garrick was drowned when his barque the "Amazon" was blown ashore onto Margam Sands at the end of August

1908. There were only two survivors from the wreck - the Captain, five apprentices and 15 crewmen were all lost. The "Amazon" public house in Port Talbot commemorates this tragic event.

RED PATH (lost)

Before the building of Church Avenue in the 1880s, a pathway had been laid between Clive Place (now Clive Road) and Church Place South. This replaced an older unmade path that stretched across the fields to the right of the new path. It has now been built over with houses. Both paths skirted a large quarry to the left (also now built on), and the older of the two was known as the Red Path. This was because there was a layer of red marl just below the topsoil, and this would have been exposed in wet weather. The new path inherited the name.

In 1892 the Local Board received numerous letters about the state of the Red Path, including one that complained "... the Red Path, from Clive Road to the Church is utterly unfit for walking, especially in wet weather", while another correspondent wrote "... [it is] unfit for walking and it should not be thrown open for wheeled traffic"[144].

In the 1890s the Local Board laid a metalled road with a flight of steps at the northern end. It made no allowance for vehicular use, and Church Avenue is still pedestrians only.

RED TRIANGLE CLUB (lost)

This Boy's Club was housed in a large single storey wooden building in the lane that leads from Fairfield Road to the Dingle Station. It was opened after the First World War and closed after the Second. It catered for boys from the working class areas of the town and provided excellent facilities, especially during theDepression of the 1930s. It gave the boys the opportunity to play football and table-tennis and to box. The Club turned out many notable boxers, including John 'Buster' Jones. Woodworking, dancing and other skills were also taught. The Club was run for many years by the late Percy Cotton, a man held in the highest esteem by all who knew him.

Film shows were another popular feature. The author saw his first films at the Club during the Second World War, including a couple of Charlie Chaplin

---

[144] Penarth Observer, 1892.

short features. The club was built up on "stilts" as the site was an old dried out watercourse, the route, in fact, of the stream that used to run alongside today's Grove Terrace before flowing into the Windsor Dingle. The Club was demolished to build homes, although a short section of the watercourse could still be seen right up until the time tipping took place to prepare a site for the subsequent Air Corps Hall, which has itself now been rebuilt.

REGAL

In November 1906 the Plymouth Estates leased a plot of land to a company known as the Paget Rooms Company Ltd. The company built a large hall with a small shop on either side of the frontage. The hall was named the Paget Rooms in honour of the Earl of Plymouth who had married Alberta Paget in 1883. During the 1930s it became a cinema. Run by the Willmore Brothers, it was rechristened the Regal, although it was not a success, perhaps because of its flat floor, which made it difficult for people at the back to see. It subsequently became a public hall and a popular dance hall.

In 1950 it was acquired by the Penarth Urban District Council.

REVES

The Reves was another Norman foreshore fishery around Penarth. It was rented out and is referred to in numerous official records, including Minister's Account to the Crown for 1433-34. The exact location of the Reves is as yet unknown. Other fisheries included the Balle and the Brodefiord.

RICHARD'S LANE (lost)

Penarth's most famous cobbled and stepped street, Hill Street, was originally shown on the 1859 map of the town as Richard's Lane. As is the case with the nearby Powell's Lane, the derivation is uncertain. However an Edward Priests Richards was the Cardiff-based agent of the Marquess of Bute during the period 1825-1865 and was described by George Robinson in 1859 as "the central pivot round whom revolved the whole Bute planetary system".

RIDGEWAY (lost)

The Penarth Ridge runs from Penarth Head west to Cogan Pill, and the original Docktown was built on the ridge in the 1850s. It would appear there was an

The 'Pilot' at the top of the steps of Hill Street originally 'Richard's Lane.

early path across the ridge, possibly dating from Roman times when it might have been a link with an observation post and watch tower on the cliff edge at Penarth Head.

G.O.Pierce cites the earlier versions Rigewei - "viam vocatem Rigewei, early 14th century" and Rydgway (le). He suggests wei and way are derived from the Old English weg, meaning a way, a path, a road[145]. There would certainly have been a path leading to the parish church, which had been built in the 12th century.

RIVER SUBWAY

The Penarth Dock opened in 1865, most of the dock workers, known as dock labourers, came from the Grangetown and Cardiff areas. (The title 'Docker' came much later.)

The river Ely used to be crossed in the small packet ship, the "Conquerer", owned by M.R.Clements, a Cardiff engineer. This was in operation between 1857 and 1865, when it was replaced by a steam-driven chain ferry. The Cardiff Steam Navigation Company ran their steamer, the "Kate", built by John Payne of Bristol, on a route from Cardiff Dock to Penarth Dock between 1865 and 1867, when the vessel was bought by Valentine Trayes (see Northcliff).

In the early years of the 1890s plans were drawn up to drive a tunnel/subway under the River Ely. Work started in 1897 and was finished in early 1900. The subway was opened to the public on 14 May 1900.[146] The toll was one old penny for pedestrians, twopence for a bicycle, and fourpence for a pram. The owners of the Taff Vale Railway actually issued railway tickets. The subway closed in 1963.

There were substantial red-brick entrance buildings at both ends of the subway. There was a toll-keeeper's office at the Grangetown end and the Penarth Dock Police Office at the Penarth end. The Penarth building has gone, although the Grangetown one is still standing, in excellent condition, on Mud Point.

ROCKET HOUSE AND CARRIAGE HOUSE

The town's second Coastguard accommodation block and station were built in 1864. As well as the cottages and a watch tower,there were two other buildings,

[145] G O Pierce, ibid.
[146] R. Thorne, ibid.

the Rocket and Carriage houses. These beautiful examples of Victorian building are still, fortunately, with us - two little gems, standing in the narrow alley that links Tower Hill with Holmesdale Place.

The Rocket House contained a form of mortar that fired a long line from the cliff or foreshore out to a stricken or disabled vessel. The apparatus was drawn along on a four-wheeled carriage which was hauled by the rocket team who would have been harnessed to the carriage rather like horses. A team comprised either 4 or 6 men.

On 10 December 1891, the large four-masted barque, the "Drumblair" an iron vessel weighing 1,907 tons, and measuring 267 feet long and 40 feet wide, which had been built by Russel and Co., left Barry heading for Port Pierre, Mauritius, carrying a cargo of coke. A west-by-south west gale blew up, and battling against heavy seas the vessel was driven back up the Channel before being stranded on the western side of Sully Island. A steam tug which had unsuccessfully attempted to connect up with the Drumblair came to tow the Penarth lifeboat, the Joseph Denman II, to the scene. By the time the lifeboat arrived both the Barry and Penarth Rocket Teams were already in attendance[147]. The vessel and crew were all eventually saved. The coxwain of the lifeboat was Declan Kenure who lived in Maughan Street.

ROCK VILLA (lost)

This large and handsome semi-detatched villa, one of a pair along with Balcony Villa, was built on the Promenade in the 1860s and was at various times used as a private residence and a guest house. Both the villas had an enclosed balcony running along their entire frontage at first floor level. In appearance they were very similar to some of the houses overlooking Barry Old Harbour.

The census of 1881 showes the owner/occupier as a Mrs Matthews, who was living there with her niece and one servant.

ROGERSMOORE

The name Roger is well evidenced in and about Penarth. Pierce cites Coed Cati-Rosser and Roger's Hook at Leckwith, Rogers Cwm Way, Wenvoe, and

---

[147] G. Farr: Shipwreck of the Sea.

Rogersmoor Wood at Penarth[148]. Who Roger was remains a mystery, however. The earliest reference appears to be Rogers More in 1540, although a later Roger's Moor appears in 1700.

The moor was part of the Penarth Plateau. A marshy area, it is now encompassed by Archer Road, Westbourne Road, Lavernock Road and Stanwell Road. It used to run south from the West Moor. Evenlode School can be identified as the centre of Roger's Moor.

The derivation could well be from Roger Gramus (c.1180) who donated land to the monks of Margam Abbey. He held numerous holdings in the southern part of Glamorgan. There are no further references to the name Gramus after around 1312.

ROGER'S MOOR FARM

This farm stood on the site of today's Evenlode School, and we know there was certainly a farm here at around the turn of the 18th century. In 1720 the land was being farmed by John Phillips who held the mineral rights to "alibaster [sic] and limestone on the cliff of the sea[149]. In 1811 it is recorded as being occupied by Dan Rees and covering an area of 22 acres. As recently as 1881 it was occupied by a farmer named John Thorne. The 1881 Census shows that John and Mary Thorne, together with their three sons William, Watkin and Frederick, were in resident, along with Henry and Charles Smith, who were described as brothers-in-law. There was also a Mr W. Bray, a guest, and Edward Lichfield, a farm labourer, and his wife Eliza.

The farm covered 69 acres with the sea cliff forming its eastern-most extremity. A limekiln is shown on old Ordnance Survey maps roughly at the end of what is now Craven Walk.

Dressed stone found near the school is reputed to be the last remains of the farm. It could, however, be stone from the stone-dressing operations at the Cwrt-y-Vil quarries during the 19th century.

ROGER'S MOOR WOOD

This dense wood was roughly in the middle of Roger's Moor and was later bisected when Victoria Road was built in the 1880s. The two areas of the wood

[148] G O Pierce, ibid.
[149] Bute Papers.

were felled and cleared to provide land for housing, but fortunately a few mature trees still remain in the gardens of these more recent houses. One cannot but feel sad, however, to remember what a glorious wood this must have been at one time.

They must have been a wonderful playground, replete with wild life. Mr Rowlands[150] recalls that nightingales visited the woods every year during the 19th century, which stirred up a lot of local interest. He also tells how on one occasion a gorilla was believed to have found its way to the darkest depths of the wood, although it turned out to be no more than a braying donkey!

RONECH (LOST)

This appears to be the earliest known name for Steep Holm and is shown on various early documents, including the Liber Landavensis[151] The island certainly was inhabited from around AD 410. A number of early Welsh Saints, including St. Cadoc and St. Gildas, used it as anchorites, and during Norman times a priory was established on this bleak rock.

ROSEBERY PLACE

Originally known as Caroline Place and renamed Rosebery Place at the turn of the century in honour of Lord Rosebery, who was the British Prime Minister in 1894. Lord Rosebery, who during his early days was plain Archibald Primrose, was at Oxford with John, Third Marquess of Bute, and later, as the Fifth Earl of Rosebery, he paid a touching tribute at the annual meeting of the Scottish History Society following the death his old friend.

ROUND PITT (LOST)

In 1766 Round Pitt comprised a large nine acre field directly behind West House Farm. At this time the farm was owned by Catherine Edwards and it was the largest farm in the parish. It totalled 219 acres and had fields scattered throughout the parish, including Breaches Field (now the site of the Police Station and surrounding houses), Callaf's Field which is now the site of the High View Estate, and Callaf's Wood, the heavily wooded land that turns left from High View.

---

[150] Rowlands, ibid.
[151] Liber Landavensis.

ROYAL OAK (LOST)

The Royal Oak in one of Penarth's lost public houses. E T Bevan[152] has it as being on the corner of Salop Street and Albert Road and in operation during the 19th century. Given the fact that it must have been much frequented by dock workers it is strange that no evidence has yet been found to substantiate this claim. A more probable site would have been the Hong Kong.

ROXBURGH

This fine house, demolished to make way for the building of Roxburgh Court, was built for J. Pyke Thompson in the early 1880s, when it was known as Redlands. During the 1880s S A Brain, the brewer, originally lived at a house called Roxburgh in Roath Road, Cardiff (now Newport, Road), but in 1885 he moved to another Roxburgh, this one in Park Road, Penarth. He remained there until 1899, when he moved to the house originally known as Redlands but which he renamed Roxburgh.

A Miss Brain ran a private school from Roxburgh, Park Road, for a few years during the 1880s and 90s.

SABRINA

Penarth lines on the western shore of the Severn Sea, which is fed by the River Severn. The Romans knew the River Severn as the Sabrina, and indeed it may well have been known by that name for many years before even they occupied the area.

The name derives from ancient folklore. Sabrina was the illegitimate daughter of King Lochrine and his mistress, Estrildus, a beautiful German girl who had been captured when Lochrine and his brothers, Kamber and Albanactus, defended the Huns under their chief, Humber. Lochrine's Queen, Gwendolen, the daughter of Corineus, discovered their liaison and raised an army against her husband in Cornwall. She fought a battle against Lochrine and his army close to the River Stour. The King was killed by an arrow, and Gwendolen ordered that Estrildis and Sabrina be thrown into the river. From that time on the river was known as Sabrina in English and Habren (now Hafren) in Welsh. The name was still in common use right up until Norman times.

---

[152] E. T. Bevan, ibid.

The famous playwright Milton knew of the legend and Sabrina appears in his masque 'Comus' where she is described as "The guiltless damsel flying in mad pursuit of her enraged stepdam Gwendolen ..... And [she] underwent a quick immortal change, made Goddess of the river". Sabrina is also used in reference to the river in the Latin manuscripts of Tacitus, St. Gildas and Bede.

As late as the 16th century the river was still referred to as the Sabrina. It is shown as such on a map of the British Isles printed in Rome in 1546 and attributed to George Lily[153].

SALISBURY CLUB (LOST)

The Salisbury Club was yet another of the town's numerous drinking clubs and during the 1880s and 90s occupied the site of what is today the Penarth Ex-Servicemen's Club in Windsor Road. In the 1890s its manager was J. H. Lovegrove. The present site has been greatly changed and enlarged.

SALOP STREET

According to the 1859 Town Plan, Salop Street was one of the town's original thoroughfares as were Ludlow Street, Arcot Street, Maughan Street, John Street and Plassey Street. It is yet another reminder of the Windsor-Clive-Plymouth dynasty. Salop (or Shropshire) was the home county of Robert Clive, Baron Plassey, who was born in Market Drayton, the eldest son of Richard Clive, Member of Parliament for the Montgomeryshire Boroughs. The Clive family settled in Salop during the reign of Henry II and took their name from the Clive estate where they made their home. The family eventually went on to own many estates throughout the county - see also Bromfield Place, Craven Walk, etc.

SALTER'S FIELD (LOST)

This was a more recent name for the general area known by the umbrella title 'the Billybanks', and was in common use up until the end of the war. Once the quarrying activities came to an end the area was used as rough grazing for cows, donkeys and horses, as well as for pig and chicken breeding.

[153]   F. J. North, Glamorgan History, Volume 2.

The derivation could well go back to the Salter family who ran various businesses in the town and on the seafront. They bought the Penarth Mews from the Andrews family in the early years of this century. It may well have been that they used the Billybanks to graze their own horses, hence the reference to Salter.

SAMMELIS WERE (LOST)

One of the fish weirs on the River Ely during early Norman times, Sammelis Were is now lost and its exact location is not known. (See also Middlewere and Nirwere). Neither can be traced although it is likely it was at some time leased by a man called Sammel. A tenuous case, however, might also be made for Sammel to be a corruption of salmon in the old local dialect.[154]

SAINT'S SCHOOLS

During the nineteenth century the town was home to dozens of small private schools, many of which were named after a saint. These included:

Saint Audries, where the Principal was a Miss Frost, and which operated from 33 Plymouth Road;

Saint Charles Catholic School for Girls, owned and run by Mrs Charles Jones during the 1880s and 90s from variously 26, 28 and 48 Clive Place. This school, incidentally, had close links with a Boy'sSchool established in 1886 and run by Mr Charles Jones at 2 Albert Crescent. The boys' school continued in business until 1905 when the house was demolished to make way for Albert Road Methodist Church, whereupon the boys moved to the Penarth Tutorial College which operated until 1910 from 9 and 10 Stanwell Road;

St. Frideswydes School, where the Principals were a Miss Sessions and a Miss Wylde. This operated from 12 Victoria Road and later became St. Alma's, now part of Westbourne School;

---

[154] Paterson, 1492.

St. Maeburn's Ladies School, meanwhile, opened in 1886 in Marine Parade. Its Co-Principals were Miss Bates and Miss Sumner.

SARDIS

Sardis was the name given to the Presbyterian Chapel opened in Plassey Street on 18 September 1861. It was only recently demolished and replaced by an elegant Meeting House for the Jehovah's Witnesses. It was the first consecrated building in the modern town to be used for religious services, pre-dating the present Saint Augustine's Church by five years virtually to the day. (St. Augustines, 'the Top Church' as it was known, was opened on 11 September 1866.)

Prior to the building of Sardis, the Presbyterians, also known as he Calvinistic Methodists, met in various venues, including the barn of one Farmer Lawrence whose farm was on the site of what is now Lloyds Bank. The Presbyterians now meet at St. Davids in Elfed Avenue which was opened in 1954.

SEAMEN'S MISSION AND READING ROOM

When Penarth Dock closed on 6 July 1936, the grand Mission to Seamen building became superfluous to requirements. The Mission had been opened on 19 October 1878 by Lord Windsor as part of the celebrations held to mark his coming of age on 27 August 1878. It was closed and taken over by the Dock Board (Great Western Railway) who used it for various activities and purposes, particularly when the Dock was reopened following the outbreak of the war in 1939.

When the Mission closed in 1936, an alternative building was needed to cater for seamen serving on vessels using the Pontoon and the Tidal Harbour, which at that time was still busy. To meet this demand, a large single storey building was erected at the entrance to the Dock at Cogan, and this is still standing. The building is today used by the Cogan Old Age Pensioners.

Entrance to the Dock was gained under a road bridge and through a long tunnel, both of which are excellent examples of Victorian engineering. These, however, have now been closed and blocked off as a result of the Cardiff Bay redevelopment scheme.

SEARCHLIGHT STEPS

When the Penarth Head Fort was built during the last years of the 19th century to defend Cardiff and Penarth Docks from the risk of sea-borne attack, two huge searchlights were installed to light up the seaward approaches. The searchlights, in their massively constructed cast iron casings, were sited on platforms standing high above the foreshore on a trellis work of 16 tall concrete legs. The platforms were then linked by means of a narrow walkway.

The platforms were connected to the Head Fort by another narrow walkway leading from the platforms to the cliff face, and then up an almost vertical, zig-zag stairway comprising hundreds of concrete steps. The steps and platforms were flattened by a massive cliff fall in the early 1960s. However, the diligent searcher can still find remains of both the installation and the steps strewn along the foreshore or partially buried at the foot of the cliff directly below Penarth Head.

SEAVIEW

Seaview was built in the 1860s in Bradford Place for Mr Vachell, a brick manufacturer, but was eventually demolished whereupon the site was used for the building of Seaview Court, a large complex of apartments.

This town mansion, with its beautiful interior, was set in large well-tended gardens and for the last three decades of the 19th century and the first three of this one it was the home of the wealthy shipowner John Cory and his family. In 1892 Cory had an extensive stabling block built to replace the smaller original. All that remains of Seaview today is a section of the original boundary wall. Just before it was demolished it was being used as a Children's Home.

The 1871 Census records Edwin Vachell, his wife Anne, a governess, a cook and a housemaid being in residence.

SHAKESPEARE ROAD (LOST)

The houses in what is now Hastings Avenue originally stood in Shakespeare Road. Building started in the late 1920s and in 1927 the road consisted of just two houses - Archie Boland lived in one and F G Fielding lived in the other.

Searchlight platforms and the 'Searchlight Steps'.

By 1929, just two years later, there were 46 houses and the name was changed to Hastings Avenue at around the same time.

SHIP HOTEL

One of the town's first public houses, the Ship Hotel was built in the 1850s. This large building, which was constructed of bathstone, stood at the junction of Glebe Street and Maughan Street. It had an impressive frontage, including three highly decorative balconies at first floor level. The ground floor to the southern end was occupied by the first chemist in Penarth, Richard Proctor.

It had an infamous reputation, being used by seamen and members of the darker side of the town's society, and can justifiably be regarded as the heart of Daggertown. In 1869, Inspector Adams of the Glamorgan Police was called to attend a fracas at the Ship Hotel. Three drunken seamen (two Malays and an Englishman) together with a local woman of doubtful reputation were trying to force entry against the wishes of the landlord, William Richards. The Inspector arrived with two constables and in the ensuing melée Adams was stabbed just below the heart. The Police returned to their station at the double, where they armed themselves with cutlasses before returning to the fray. They were at this point joined by Henry Lovett, an ex-army officer and owner of the Windsor Hotel and Brewery. Having rushed back to the Ship Hotel, yet another fight followed in which Lovett was also stabbed. The seamen and the woman were arrested. Happily, both Adams and Lovett recovered from their injuries.

With the decline of the Dock, the pub eventually closed its doors, as did the Dock Hotel and the Marine Hotel. During the Second World War the old Ship Hotel was used to accommodate European refugees, mainly Belgians who had made the sea crossing and landed at Penarth Dock. After the war the Ship Hotel was demolished and the Catherine Meazey flats were built on the site.

Soloman Andrews bought up three small companies operating horse-drawn buses between Cardiff and Penarth in the early 1870s. One of these was owned by Richards & Price, who ran an hourly service from the Ship Hotel to St. Marys Street in Cardiff.

SPION KOP (LOST)

This was the name used for the largest of the heaps of spoil at the Billybanks. It was situated between Limekiln Cottages and the lime kilns themselves. The name comes from the Afrikaans kopje, meaning a peak. Like the name Dardanelles, it was brought back by servicemen who had seen action abroad, in this case those returning from the Boer Wars in South Africa.

The Kop used to have a deep depression at its summit and this was used by the local (and illegal) 'pitch and toss' school. The gamblers would use the younger Bowery Boys to act as look-outs, and they were drilled to yell a warning if one of the local policemen appeared. Appropriately enough, the Afrikaans name Spion Kop translates as Spy Peak or Lookout Hill.

SEVEN SISTERS

The paved cliff walk used to end just beyond what is today Stanton Way, but in earlier years there used to be a small copse of trees growing here and these were known as the Seven Sisters. Local legend has it that this was the scene of black magic rites.[155]

SOUTH PIER (LOST)

The entrance to Penarth Dock was protected by two massively built wooden piers, one to the north and one to the south. The South Pier was used on the Penarth Motor Boat Club's regatta days.

One ever-popular form of entertainment was to try to climb out to the end of the "greasy pole" which projected out from the pier. There was always fierce rivalry among the Bowery Boys to see who could achieve this, although the best prize most of those taking part could hope for was a ducking in the murky depths of the sea.

Both piers have now been demolished, although the stumps of the South Pier can still be seen at low water.

STAIRS

Just to the north of the Seven Sisters there is a range of man-made steps hewn out of the cliff face and known as the Stairs. They are used in particular by fishermen as a shortcut to the foreshore but they are very dangerous in wet weather.

---

[155] Oral tradition.

The name has a historic basis since the rock formation on the foreshore at the foot of the Stairs has also been known as the Stairs for many years, certainly since the middle of the 19th century. Paterson refers to them as Robinson's Stairs, possibly a reference to George Robinson, a well-known Radical in Cardiff in the early 19th century and an active opponent of the Bute 'Castle party'[156].

STANTON WAY

This is apparently yet another reference to the many estates owned by the Windsor-Clive family, this one being a reference to Stanton Lacey in Shropshire.

STANWELL ROAD

Stanwell Road was originally known as Parish Road, and ran from what is today Lavernock Road up as far as the parish church of St. Augustine's. In 1880 the Local Board decided to change the name of the section between "the Railway Bridge [and] the top of the hill" to Stanwell Road. Later still, in 1889, another section stretching from Windsor Road to Stanwell Crescent (which had been built in 1887) became Albert Road.

The derivation of Stanwell Road can be traced right back to the earliest recorded ancestor of the Windsor family, the great Norse Viking explorer "Othere, the old sea captain who dwelt in Helgoland"[157] who is commemorated as the discoverer of the North Cape in the appendix to King Alfred's translation of Orosius, later put into verse by the American poet Henry Wadsworth Longfellow:

> "His hair was yellow as hay,
> Hearty and hale was Othere".

Othere had settled in England, even though he was a man of substance and wealth in his native Helgoland:

> "I have six hundred reindeer, with sheep and swine, I have tribute from the Finns"[158].

156 Ibid.
157 W. P. Williams: Windsor Monograph. 1878.
158 Ibid.

It is from this redoubtable man that the Windsors are descended. He made his home and established his power base at Stanwell on the north bank of the River Thames between what is now Staines and Old Windsor in around AD 900. His grandson, Other, held vast estates in five counties under Edward the Confessor -Middlesex, Berkshire, Hampshire, Buckinghamshire and Surrey. His son Walter, Othere's great-grandson, assumed the name de Windsor and eventually became Baron and Castellaine of Windsor in 1194. His son William in turn became William de Windsor, Lord Stanwell.

STEEP HOLM

This name for the island reminds us of the Viking occupation of the island during the two or three centuries immediately before the Norman occupation. Holm is derived from the old Norse holmr meaning a river island. In the year AD 914 ten Viking vessels led by two Jarls (the equivalent of our earls) attacked a number of coastal towns in Somerset. After looting, raping and burning in and around Watchet "... they hastily set sail to their stronghold on the island of Steepholm and later sailed off to Ireland".[159]

The island was at various times home to a Roman signal station, a medieval priory, a hermitage, a farm, cottages and an inn. A small stone harbour had been built on its eastern side. The harbour itself was built between 1831 and 1832. The Reverend John Skinner visited Steepholm in 1832 and reported that '..... owing to the carelessness of the man at the helm [of a hired sailing boat] we ran onto the shingle bank outside the little harbour[160]. And excellent water colour by M. A. Sweeting produced in around 1858 shows the harbour with boats moored inside. This is used as the frontispiece for the Rendell's book on Steepholm.

The harbour was destroyed by gales later in the nineteenth century. Its site, however, can still be traced at low water and numerous large dressed stones can be identified - the remains of the old harbour walls.

In more recent times it has been an Army establishment, the site of a coastal battery and an anti-aircraft battery.

STEPAN RELICE (ALSO STEOPAN REOLICE)

These two names appear on early documents, various legal and ecclesiastical records as well as in the Anglo-Saxon Chronicles. The word stepan/steopan

[159] G. Farr: Somerset Harbours. Ibid.
[160] Ibid.

comes from the Old English steep, while relice/reolice appears to come from the Old Irish reilig, meaning a cemetery and/or the Latin reliquiae or relics. Numerous graves and skeletons have been found on both Steep Holm and Flat Holm. Steep Holm was used by Irish sea raiders at various times of its history, especially during and immediately after the last years of the Roman occupation. It was later also used by the Vikings and subsequently by the early Welsh Saints and their acolytes.

During the 12th century a priory was established on the island and dedicated to St. Michael. In an edict, Richard I decreed the provision of: "...perpetual alms to St. Michael's of Steepholm and the Brothers there serving God"[161].

The first Prior was William, and he was attended by 12 canons and a number of lay brothers at the Priory built on this isolated and desolate carboniferous limestone island. A court record dated 1243 shows that "Brother Gregory and Brother Robert of la Houme" were accused of larceny and found guilty[162].

STERSHOUSE (LOST)

G O Pierce[163] records two early references - one to the Stershouse (1540-41) and the other to the Stertehouse (1542). He suggests the derivation is from the Old English steort which means a tail or tongue of land. It could well have referred to the tongue-shape shingle promontory that ran north from the site of the Penarth Head Inn. This was lost with the excavations for the Dock Entrance.

The beach has been used from the earliest times for the loading and unloading of vessels, especially by pirates and smugglers. It is quite probable, then, that a warehouse or storehouse could have been sited on the landward side of the promontory.

In the 1850s the town's first recognized boat builder's yard was established on the tail or tongue by two men, messrs. Hambly and Fifoot[164]. This yard was closed when work started on the dock excavations in 1859. Hambly and Fifoot built pilot cutters called yawls, small barges, and the ubiquitous Bristol Channel Trading Smacks, now all lost.

---

[161]   John and Stan Rendell: Steepholm. 1993. Ibid.
[162]   Rendell, ibid.
[163]   G. O. Pierce, ibid.
[164]   Cardiff Directory, 1855. Ibid.

ST. DAVID'S CHURCH

By the 1880s/1890s the town's High Church-High Tory ruling clique was becoming increasingly concerned about the spread of non-conformity in both religious and political life which was being spearheaded by the emerging middle class. A classic example of this new radicalism was the Wesleyan, Mr W B Gibbs, who on 4 March 1892 asserted "he was proud of his position, identifying him as it did with the Liberal and progressive party of Penarth". A few months later,on 1 July 1892 Gibbs said he "... had been asking himself why he was a Liberal and a Radical, [and] it was because he was discontented at there being one law for the rich and one for the poor"[165].

To combat the spread of this non-conformity two new Anglican Churches were planned and built in the 1890s. All Saints was the first, being consecrated on 31 October 1893. St. David's (now Holy Nativity) was the second, and this was consecrated by the Bishop of Llandaff on 29 January 1894.

The plans for St. Davids were presented to the Local Board in the first week of August 1892. The church was designed to hold 370 people at worship. It was to be sited at the junction of New Plassey Street and Windsor Road. New Plassey Street at that time stretched from High Street to Windsor Road, the two sections, that is to say the original and the new, being renumbered in October 1895 and becoming known simply as Plassey Street. Just before it was consecrated, a decision was taken to give the church the name it is known by today, Holy Nativity.

SULLY

G O Pierce[166] states the origin of the name Sully is obscure and that the earliest evidence is in the 12th century. He suggests the name could have been introduced to the area by the de Sully family, perhaps Walter de Suli (1193-8). Paterson[167] meanwhile suggests the name comes from the Old Norse sul, meaning something which is cleft and furrowed, and the Old Norse ey or island (compare Ramsey, Caldy, Anglesey etc.) When viewed from the sea, the island with its raised eastern and western ends, does indeed give the impression of a clef or furrow. The eastern end shows remains of Iron and Bronze Age occupation and early Ordnance Survey maps of the area show a "Danish" camp

---

[165] Penarth Observer.
[166] Pierce, ibid.
[167] Paterson, ibid.

or fort. Certainly the Vikings used the island as a place to repair their longships.

The first holders of the Manor of Sully were followers of Robert Fitzhamon. The Carta Glamorgania refers to Walter de Sulia, Sheriff, in about 1190, who brought a well-documented lawsuit against Pagan de Tuberville. De Sulia held Knights Fees for Coity, Coychurch, Sully, Leckwith and he shared Llanmaes with Gilbert de Constantin (see Cosmeston). Walter's son, also named Walter, held two Knights Fees at Sully in the 1250s, two at Wenvoe and a share in Llanmaes. Reimond de Sully, c.1299, was closely associated with the de Clare family, especially the notorious Bogo de Clare, younger brother of Gilbert de Clare, the Red Earl.

The manor was held from 1780 until 1812 by Sir John de la Fountaine Tyrwhit, the family later taking the name Drake.

SWANBRIDGE

Having their base on the virtually tree-less islands of Flat Holm and Steep Holm, which also lacked supplies of fresh water, the Vikings used Sully Island to repair their longships. Both the Holms had very small landing beaches, quite unsuitable for boat repairs. Sully, though, had fresh water, a long sheltered shingle beach, and an easily attainable supply of timber from Hopkin Mount, the hillock just behind what is now the Captain's Wife public house.

Sweyn Forkbeard, the Viking Jarl who founded Sweyn's Ey or Swansea, used Sully Island and it would seem that Swanbridge is a corruption of Sweyn's Brygga, brygga being Old Norse for a causeway or bridge, as in Fileybrig and Brighouse, both in another Viking stronghold, Yorkshire. Nearer to home there is a series of caves on the Gower Coast which are known colloquially as Sweyn's Houses. Laurence Nowch's map of Wales, produced in around 1570, shows a Swan Sey.

SWASHWAYS

This was the name given to a stretch of the River Ely roughly between the Upper and Lower Fords (fjords), just off Mud Point[168]. It is now the site of the Penarth Motor Boat and Sailing Club. The name was lost with the building of the Docks.

---

[168] Smythe, ibid.

SWIMMING BATHS

The Penarth (Large and Small) Swimming Baths were housed in an elegant Victorian building with an unusual cupola surmounted by a leaping dolphin. A domed tower of Russian complexity of outline, with an iron trimmed roof with decorative scrollwork. They were opened in 1885 having been built to the designs of H G Harris and H Snell, Surveyor and Architect respectively to the Windsor Estates and the Local Board. The cost of £7,500 was met by Lord Windsor and the Local Board.

Two reservoirs were built in the Alexandra Gardens to hold salt water which was pumped up from under the Pier at high water. The cast iron intake can still be seen under the pier. The Baths were converted to use fresh water some years before they were closed.

The Baths were closed after the Leisure Centre was built at Cogan on the site of the Cogan Pill Tile and Brick Works. After years of civic neglect, the original plan was for the Baths to be demolished and the site redeveloped. Fortunately, as the result of detailed architectural and historical research and a vociferous public campaign, the building was saved and classed as a Grade II listed building. They have been sympathetically converted into a popular public house known as the "Inn at the Deep End".

'TABS'

'Tabs' is the familiar name by which the Baptist Movement's Tabernacle in Plassey Street is known.

The first record of Baptists in the town is in 1858 when Mr Samuel White, a local grocer, attended a service held in a cottage in Glebe Street being conducted by a lay preacher. By 1864, a carpenter's loft in Chapel Lane was being used for Baptist services.

In 1869 a Building Committee was established, and they soon identified a site on the corner of Arcot Street and Plassey Street. In a move motivated as much by politics as by religion, Lady Clive offered them an out of town site (the exact location is not known). But being regarded as too far off the beaten track offer, her offer was declined. The present site was eventually acquired, and the Foundation Stone was laid on 14 September 1870 by Richard Cory Junior. The first service of worship was held in the Chapel on Sunday, 10 May 1871.

The original building, which cost £1,000 to erect, was 56 feet long and 36 ft wide, and could seat 270 people. In 1894 it was rebuilt and enlarged, finally

PENARTH BATHS

Penarth Swimming Baths now the 'Inn at the Deep End'.

re-opening its doors to worshippers on Wednesday, 20 November 1895. The cost of the new work was £3,000.

The 'Tabs' building has recently been extended, refurbished and modernised under the leadership of its Pastor, John James. It has now become a vibrant and thriving religious and community centre.

TAYLOR'S FARM

This was one of the many farms that used to exist in the parish of Penarth before urbanization, but was eventually lost as the town developed. It used to stand where Plymouth Road meets Stanwell Road, roughly on the site of the current National Westminster Bank. The 1841 Census shows John Taylor, who was 90 at the time, as the farmer in residence, along with his wife and their son, also called John, a grandson and one servant. John Taylor senior died at the ripe old age of 100 in 1850 and is buried in St. Augustine's Churchyard. The Censuses of 1851, 1861 and 1871 all show John Taylor junior as continuing to farm the land. The farm was eventually demolished in about 1880.

TOP CHURCH

The Top Church was the colloquial name for St. Augustine's Church, which was constructed on the site of an early Norman church that used to grace Penarth Head. The church acted as both a land mark and a sea mark. Sir S. R. Glynne, a noted antiquarian, visited Penarth in 1853 and commented, '..... a small church very conspicuously situated on an eminence overlooking the Bristol Channel, and is a well known sea-mark'[169].

The original church was built by William Saltmarsh, the Prior of St. Augustine's, Bristol, and Bishop of Llandaff. Osbert de Pennard bequeathed the land now known as the Parish of Penarth to the Canons of St. Augustine in 1183. Saltmarsh went on to become Lord of the Manor, whereupon he had the church erected. It was demolished in 1864 and rebuilt in 1865/6.

The Top Church was designed by William Butterfield and constructed in stone in the Early English style. It cost £10,000 to build, and was paid for by the Baroness Windsor. The church comprises a chancel, nave, aisles, transepts, a porch at the north west corner, and a 96 feet high tower. It has a saddle-back roof and a fine peal of six bells '... which can be heard for many miles

[169]   Sir S. R. Glynne: Older Welsh Churches. 1903.

St. Augustine's Church, 'Top Church'. Burial place Joseph Parry.

seaward[170]'. The east window is stained and the south transept contains a single stained window, '..... given by the late Lady Windsor to commemorate her first and last visit to Penarth[171].' Above the nave arches can be seen eight circular Beatitudes. The church can seat almost 1,000 people.

TROLLEY LINES

In the 1860s a quarry was established in the area now covered by the houses of Bevan's Row and Powys Road. By the 1870s quarrying operations had also started a little further along Lavernock Road in an area bounded by what is now Lavernock Road, Dinas Road, Beechwood Drive and Purcell Road. Just two decades later the quarry covered a much larger area and included a lime kiln and three tramways.

These tramways met up at roughly where the Old Penarthians have their rugby club today, and used to cross Lavernock Road into fields now built over by the Cherwell Road development. A single tramway then ran to Westbourne Road, where it ended just below the junction with Archer Road. The fields became known as the Trolley Lines.

Quarrying operations continued right up until the First World War. The stone used to be transferred from the quarry, across Lavernock Road, where it was dressed in a series of buildings that stood approximately where today's Evenlode School has been built. The route of the tramway, the Trolley Lines, could still be seen until Cherwell Road and its neighbouring roads were built and the grounds of Evenlode School were landscaped.

The Trolley Lines field was a favourite place for the Bowery Boys to play epic games of football matches that would go on all day. Hordes of youngsters would gravitate from the North Ward and appear and disappear again as if by magic. Teams with as many as twenty or even more players on each side would do battle with each other, coats laid down as goal posts. The games would result in huge scores (one memorable one went to 88 - 72!) amid constant bouts of bickering and bloody arguments about the accuracy of the scoring. These games (for which there was never any referee) would come to an abrupt end and the hordes would disperse back up to the top of town, scrumping, playing rat-a-tat-ginger, up-ending dustbins and waylaying any unfortunate private or public schoolboy who happened to cross their path.

[170] Kelly's Directory, 1884.
[171] Ibid.

Turner House, opened 1888, now an active annex of the National Museum of Water.

© Diane Mead

TURNER HOUSE

This little gem of a building is still fortunately with us. Built in 1888 for James Pyke Thompson JP in the grounds of his home, Redlands (later Roxburgh), it was used to house his collection of paintings by J M W Turner. It was subsequently opened to the public and the building now forms part of the National Museum of Wales and offers an active, wide-ranging and revolving programme of exhibitions.

TUMP (LOST)

The Welsh word twyn can be translated as hill, hillock, tump, knoll, or rising ground. The Penarth Tump was the hillock that now forms part of Queens Road, and was the site of the early iron church of St. Pauls which was erected in 1892. The Tump was also known as the Queen's Bench.

The name enjoyed common currency during the 19th century and there are numerous references to it in the Minutes of the Local Board. The houses built

159

at the beginning of Paget Road had gardens dug out of the northern slope of the Tump.

UPPERCLIFF

This fine house, demolished long ago now, was built in the 1840s (exact date unknown) and stood in splendid isolation on Penarth Head (see Artillery House).

There is some confusion surrounding its first occupant, but it could well have been a Mrs Doughton. By the 1850s the occupants were G W Nicholl, his wife and mother-in-law (Mrs Doughton), plus servants. By the mid-1860s the occupant was John Batchelor[172]. One of Batchelor's sons, Cyril, was the founder captain of the Penarth Rugby Club in 1880. The club's original headquarters were at the Kymin, which was the home of James Batchelor, Cyril's uncle[173].

The site of the original Uppercliff and its extensive grounds are now a housing estate, also known as Uppercliff.

UPPER FORD (LOST)

The name Upper Ford came from the Old Norse Upper Fjord and was used to describe a section of the River Ely between Cwtsh-y-Cwm and the Mud Point. It was lost with the building of the Dock, but is yet another reminder of the Viking presence in this area. Fjord translates as a long narrow inlet, and was in common usages certainly up until the mid 19th century.[174]

UPPER HOUSE (LOST)

Both the house and its site are now lost. The house is shown in the Register of Electors for 1844, and might have been an earlier name for Uppercliff. Certainly Uppercliff was known for a short time during the 1870s as Higher Cliff House.

[172] K. R. Batchelor: John Batchelor - the Friend of Freedom. 1975.
[173] John Musselwhite: The Butcher's Boys of Donkey Island. c. 1980.
[174] Smythe: ibid.

UPPER MARSH (LOST)

The tide fields that stretched from the northern slope of the Penarth Ridge to the original course of the River Ely were very marshy. The area running eastwards from the mouth of the Cogan Pill and halfway to Cwtsh-y-Cwm was known as the Upper Marsh, and was used for rough grazing.

The new park planned as part of the Dock redevelopment scheme will stand on part of what was the Upper Marsh. (See also Lower Marsh).

VARTEG HOUSE SCHOOL (LOST)

Yet another of the private schools that proliferated in Penarth during the 19th century, The Varteg House Boarding and Day School was based at 2 Albert Crescent (see Penarth Tutorial College). It was run by Mr Jones, and its staff included Miss Pearce, Miss Cruickshank (who taught pianoforte), and MissWahlback (who taught French and German). The house was demolished to make way for the building of Albert Road Methodist Church, which opened in 1907.

VICTORIA SCHOOL

Work on the building of the school commenced in Queen Victoria's Jubilee Year, hence the decision to honour the event by naming the school after the Sovereign. On Tuesday, 22 June 1897 the children of Albert Road School marched in procession behind the local Artillery Band down to the proposed site, where the Rector, Mr Sweet-Escott, and his wife laid the Commemorative stone. The school was originally known as the Queen Victoria School.

VICTORIA WAREHOUSES AND WHARF

The Victoria Warehouses and Wharf Number One can still be seen in remarkably good condition on Grange Point. It is best viewed from the new River Ely Bridge. The second Victoria Wharf and Victoria Warehouses Numbers Two and Three were further up the River Ely, at approximately where the modern roundabout stands at the entrance to the Windsor Quay housing estate. The estate is built on the former Windsor slipways, graving dock, grid iron and jetties.

WASHINGTON CINEMA

The Washington was opened on 4 April 1938 for the Willmore Brothers, the opening ceremony having been performed by Lt.Col. J. H. R. Downes-Powell JP, Chairman of the Penarth District Council[175]. The Willmore Brothers had opened the town's very first cinema (see Cinema Theatre) and were responsible for the design of the Washington, a beautiful example of a medium-sized cinema built as it was at the end of the Golden Age of cinema building.

Recently saved from the threat of demolition, the building has been extensively and sympathetically refurbished and reopened as an art gallery, cafe, and a series of commercial outlets.

WASHINGTON HOTEL

The Washington Hotel was opened in October 1922[176] on the site of what had previously been two large private houses at numbers 9 and 10 Stanwell Road, and these can still be seen. The hotel was owned by Captain W.H. Bevan. Bevan had been born in Montgomeryshire. He held a Master's Ticket (Square Rig) and wasa friend and nautical adviser to the extremely wealthy American couple Mr and Mrs Frederick W. Vanderbilt.

The building has now been converted into flats.

WEARDALE FARM (lost)

This farm is mentioned in the 1881 Census which shows Solomon James, a Farm Bailiff, and his wife as occupants. Exhaustive research has failed to establish the location of the farm.

WESLEY LANE

The former Wesleyan Methodist Chapel, later the Anglican Church of St.Pauls and now the Penarth Boxing Club, was built between 1863 and 1864 in Arcot Street. It has a lane running along one side of it linking Arcot Street with Glebe Street, and this in turn has a long arm that goes off at right angles to join Salop Street. The original name for these two lanes was Wesley Lane. This was later

---

[175] Penarth Times, April 1938.
[176] Penarth Times, 13 October 1922.

changed at an unknown date to the name it is known by today, Chapel Lane.

WEST GROVE

This name applies to a short row of houses in what is today Stanwell Road and facing Trinity Church. A plaque bearing the name can be seen high on the wall of the end house where Stanwell Road meets Grove Terrace.

WEST HOUSE ROAD (lost)

When the first houses were built in the early 1880s in what is now Westbourne Road they were officially known as West House Road (see Penarth Grammar School). The name was changed in about 1894.

WEST MOOR (lost)

The West Moor covered an area stretching roughly from today's Westwood (Penarth Conservative Club) and West House, across Victoria Square and down to Roger's Moor. When plans were drawn up in the early 1880s for the Stanwell Baptist Church, the site was shown as "at the West Moors".

WEST MUD (lost)

One of the many names used to describe the large area of mud that lies between the Penarth Ridge and the River Taff, alsoknown as Penarth Harbour, Penarth Flats etc, and the site of the speculative Windsor Dock development during the 1890s.

WESTWOOD COLLEGE

Westwood House had been built by James Edwards, the Dock Superintendent on the Taff Valley Railway. On his death in 1892 the house was bought by a Mr Thomas Dyke for £2,725. The Tutorial College took up residence there in 1922 where it operated under the name Westwood College. The house is now the Penarth Conservative Club. Westwood College was a private school for boys. The college, under the headmastership of D. Wyn Thomas, closed at Easter, 1944.

WESTBOURNE ROAD

The name Westbourne has two possible derivations. The first has Windsor/ Clive connections: in 1883 the Earl of Plymouth, Robert Windsor Clive, married Alberta Victoria Sarah Caroline Paget whose family home was in Petersfield, Hampshire, next to a small hamlet called Westbourne. The second possible derivation could be that it is the name of the stream, the West Bourne, that had its head at a large pond[177] next to the house known as Woodlands. Woodlands itself was demolished and is now the site of an office block for the National Farmers Union insurance company. The large pond, now filled in, is the site of the Ty-Gwyn Nursing Home.

The stream's course was down what is now Westbourne Road towards Lower Penarth before turning westwards to merge with another stream that ran down from the One, Two, Three Woods, near Downs Farm and then into the Sully Brook.

In spite of its having been culverted, the stream can still be seen as it cuts through the bottom of the gardens belonging to the bungalows in Charteris Close. "Bourne" is a variant of the old English "burn", which itself comes from the Old German "born" - a stream.

WHITE HALL FARM (lost)

G.O. Pierce[178] identifies a Whitehall in 1793, and an even earlier reference quotes the date 1700[179] at which time the farm was being worked by David Williams. In 1720 the farm's 12 acres were leased by William Phillips. Although the actual site has notso far been pinpointed, it may well have been close to what is today the junction of Westbourne Road and Victoria Road.

WINDSOR CLUB (lost)

Yet another of the town's many 19th century drinking clubs, the Windsor Club was based at the bottom of Ferry Lane. It was originally known as the Central Club, but by 1886 and by now under the ownership of John Knight it had been re-named the Windsor.

---

[177] Ordnance Survey, 1878.
[178] Pierce: ibid.
[179] Pierce: ibid.

WINDSOR DOCK (lost)

With the rapid increase in the demand for Welsh steam coal in the late 19th century, the Taff Vale Railway promoted three successive Parliamentary Bills in an attempt to build another dock in the vicinity of the Ely Tidal Harbour. This was intended to compete with the latest Bute Dock to be constructed - the Queen Alexandra Dock. The first Bill to be introduced in the 1896 session of Parliament was called the Windsor Dock Bill and it proposed the building of a dock covering 29 acres. It would have a main lock of 1.5 acres, and the site was the mud flats immediately east of the mouth of the River Ely. Opposition from Lord Bute ensured the scheme was rejected.

The next Parliamentary session saw the introduction of a second Bill, this time for a slightly smaller dock covering 26 acres but with a 2 acre lock. This too was rejected.

During the 1898 session the TVR produced plans for a 42 acre dock. This time the plan was to build a massive embankment running out eastwards from the Windsor Slipway and then south towards Penarth. This would have covered an area of the mud flats in the vicinity of where the Red House stands today and would have involved one of the bends in the River Ely. Part of the plan included the straightening of the River Ely to eliminate the ox-bow bends, an idea first mooted by Brunel half a century earlier in the 1830s.

The lock entrance would have covered a site of 2.5 acres and cut across the entrance to the Tidal Harbour, which would necessarily have ceased trading. This third Bill, however, was again rejected, and no further plans were submitted.

WINDSOR HALL CINEMA

The Willmore Brothers bought the Windsor Hall from Solomon Andrews in 1912. It had been built by the Congregationalists in 1883, but Andrews had used it as a Public Hall. The Willmore Brothers ran the hall as a cinema until about 1915, when theyopened the purpose-built Windsor Kinema, which showed films right up until the 1950s.

Much of the original Kinema, by the way, can still be seen behind the facade of Monty Smith's Garage. Another Windsor Hall stood in Salop Street in the 1870s, although very little information is as yet available as to either the relevant dates or the exact site.

WINDSOR MEWS (lost)

The Angel Mews were re-named the Windsor Mews in the early 1900s.

WINDSOR ROAD

The name of the town's main thoroughfare and shopping centre is a constant reminder of Penarth's foremost family and the one responsible for much of its building, the Windsors. The Windsor family and their associates planned and built the Ely Tidal Harbour, Penarth's genesis, the Dock, the town centre and the railway. The family, of which Othere is the first recorded ancestor, allied themselves by marriage with many of the country's leading families, including the Clives of Shropshire, the Herberts of Powis, the Lewis family of the Van, Caerphilly, the Butes and the Bridgeman family. They became a major force in the country and played a leading role in both its political and military life.

The family has had a prominent position throughout British history. William de Windsor accompanied Richard I on his invasion of Normandy in 1194 and was killed in battle; the de Windsors joined the opposition to the tyranny of King John, fought under the banners of King Edward I, II, III and IV, and did battle against the usurper, Bolingbroke, helping to wrest the crown from Richard II.

In 1513 Andrew de Windsor accompanied Henry VIII on his expedition to France and fought at the Battle of Guinegate, also known as the "Battle of the Spurs". Later William, Lord Windsor, was appointed a Commander of Queen Mary's army of 10,000 British troops sent to France to assist the Spanish armies against the French, where he was accompanied by his son, Edward. At the consequent Battle of St Quentin, the Lord Windsor, closely followed by the Lord Dudley, were the first to scale the wall and plant the Queen's banner.

Thomas, Lord Windsor, born 1591, became Admiral of the Fleet. He died leaving no male heir, and his title passed to Thomas Hickman, the son of Elizabeth Windsor and Dixie Hickman. Hickman was an ardent Royalist and fought with great courage at the Battle of Naseby on 14 June 1645. After the Restoration he was appointed Governor of Jamaica and Admiral of the West Indies in 1666, and from Jamaica he led a successful attack on Cuba.

In this century, Archer Windsor Clive was killed in action in 1914.

In 1867 a toll road was introduced by Lord Bute[180] stretching from Grangetown to Cogan and Penarth. The stretch between Cogan and the Parish

[180] Mountford & Sprinks, ibid. Roy Thorne, ibid.

Road was to become Windsor Road. In 1868 there were only three buildings in Windsor Road- the Police Station, the Windsor Hotel and the St.Fagan's Castle Inn[181]. By 1878[182] this number had risen to 17, all located on the north side between the Police Station and the Parish Road. By the 1890s the road had taken the form we recognize today.

The English Royal Family adopted the name Windsor in 1917, changing it from Saxe-Coburg due to strong anti-German feeling resulting from the Great War. King George V was the first monarch to be known by the surname Windsor.

WOLVES

Captain Smythe described the Wolves as "..... a small dangerous cluster, North West of the Flat Holm"[183]. The rocks are carboniferous limestone and dry out at low water. The derivation is unknown, although in the eighteenth and nineteenth centuries the Welsh Channel pilots referred to them as the Woolies, a corruption perhaps of St. Woolos, who visited and stayed at Llandough and Llancarvon, and who would have visited Flat Holm and perhaps Steep Holm. This explanation would also tie in with the ecclesiastical connections with Monkstone Rock (qv.).

WOODLANDS

This house and farm stood where the National Farmers Union office block stands today. It was a large house with stables and outbuildings, and had been built for Mr. D. Morgan. In the 1881 Census, D.Morgan, a farmer, is recorded as the occupant, along with his wife, son and one servant.

WORBEYSFOTE (lost)

This name first appears around the 1200s/1300s and is thought to refer to a place somewhere between Cardiff and Penarth. The confusion surrounding its exact location is compounded by a 13th century reference to Henry Worgon granting land to William Wallot "... in a place called Norden, lyingwithin the

---

[181] Waring: Penarth Map, 1868.
[182] Ordnance Survey map, 1878.
[183] Smythe, ibid.

fee [or Knightsfee], of Pennarth, between the way called Ridgewei on the south and lande of the Lord of Pennarth (Glebeland) on the west and land of the Lord of Cogan on the north and a place called Worbeysfote on the east"[184]. From this description it would appear that Worbeysfote may have been an early reference to either Cwtsh-y-Cwm or the Kymin.

Translated roughly, "worbey" is a river farm while "fote" means the foot or the lower part of the mouth of a river or stream.

WORKINGMAN'S CHURCH (lost)

This was the colloquial name for the Anglican church built in iron that used to stand on the Queens's Bench/Tump, now the site of Church Terrace, Queen's Road. The sobriquet shows the class divisions that were rife in 19th century Penarth - St. Augustines was described as the "Top Church" (qv), while this one was known as the Workingman's Church.

Between 1881 and 1891 the Church had originally stood on the corner of Rectory Road and Stanwell Road during which time it was known as All Saints. It was moved to the Tump after the present All Saints Church in Victoria Square was consecrated in October 1891.

Lord Windsor subscribed £400 towards the cost of building the church, the remaining £250 being met by the parishioners. The church could seat 400 people. Its first curate was the Rev. Richard David Lewis, M.A. of Jesus College, Oxford.

WRACH (see Cefn-y-Wrach)

YMCA

The first meeting place of the YMCA (Young Men's Christian Association) in the 19th century was at 57 Plassey St. Between 1916 and 1917 they met at premises above the Arcade which had opened as the YMCA Soldiers Club. It finally closed after the Second World War and is now used as offices.

ZIG-ZAG (lost)

This series of paths, laid as the name suggests in a zig-zag formation, were cut into the cliff face behind the Custom House and Dock Buildings. The path led

---

[184]   Paterson, ibid.

down from the grounds of the Penarth Hotel (owned by the Taff Valley Railway) and could be used by hotel guests and the general public alike. Mr Rowland noted - "I occasionally, years ago, used the path, but it was always dirty and never really safe because of water comingthrough the soil causing land slides"[185].

On 20 September 1896 George Isgar, the son of Chas Isgar, who had owned the Central Club, was out blackberrying with some friends at the Zig-Zag when he fell 100 feet down the slope. Two men, James Tonkin and Harry Brown, ran from the beach and took the boy to Dr. Aitkens's Surgery. The boy had fortunately rolled part of the way down the cliff face, although he had still suffered cuts to the head and face, bruising to the body, and been badly shaken by the experience. Fortunately, his injuries were not too serious and he made a speedy recovery.

APPENDIX

FIDDLER'S ELBOW

The first houses in Upper Cwrt-y-Vil Road were built c.1890, those in Lower Cwrt-y-Vil were built after 1896, the demarcation line between Upper and Lower was and is Archer Road. The junction between two roads was known as Fiddler's Elbow and there are two references to Fiddler's Elbow in Council Minutes for April and May 1896. Original occupants of Upper Cwrt-y-Vil included Joshua John Neale owner of Neale and West Trawlers (19 trawlers in 1914), and J.W.C. Martyr, Master Mariner, both of whom would have been indebted to Charles Crafter Couves who was the original occupant of number 1 and was designated in the Street Directory as—"patentee of a wave sub duer".

ADAM'S WOOD/ROGER'S MOOR, ROGER'S HOOK etc.

A possible derivation for these placenames could be from the de Someri family who in the 12th Century held seven knight's fees including Cogan, Dinas Powis, Llandough, Adam de Someri, or Sumeri was a contemporary of Milo de Cogan and William de Saltmarsh who was Bishop of Llandaff, 1185-1191. Adam had two sons John and Roger.

[185]   Rowlands, ibid.

169

BIBLIOGRAPHY

J. F. Andrews, *Keep Moving*, 1976.

K. R. Batchelor, *John Batchelor, the Friend of Freedom*, 1975.

E. A. Benjamin, *Penarth, 1841-1871*. 1980.

E. T. Bevan, *Old Penarth*. Unpublished manuscript kept at Penarth Library.

J. Bird, Diaries, 1790 - 1807. Edited by H. M. Thomas. 1987.

P. Carradice: *Beside the Seaside*, 1992
Headlands School, 1991
Penarth Pier, 1994.

E. Chappell, *The History of the Port of Cardiff*, 1939.

J. Davies, *Cardiff and the Marquesses of Bute*, 1981.

J. W. Dawson, *Commerce and Customs*.

H. M. Denham (Lt.), *Admiralty Survey*, 1832.

C. Evans, *Glamorgan's History and Topography*, 1943.

D. Fanning, *St. Joseph's, Penarth*. 1990.

G. Farr, *Somerset Harbours*, 1954.
West Country Passenger Steamers, 1956
Wreck and Rescue in the Bristol Channel, 1967

J. M. Gibbs, *Morels of Cardiff*, 1982
Trinity Methodist Church, Penarth, 1994

Sir S. R. Glynne, *Older Welsh Churches*. 1903

Commander R. Graham, *Rough Passage*. c.1930

Basil Greenhill, *The Merchant Schooners*. 1951.

B. Greenhill & W. Slade. *West Country Ketches*. 1974.

P. Heaton, *Welsh Blockade Runners in the Spanish Civil War*. 1985.

J. B. Hilling, *Glamorgan Historian, Volume 7*. 1971

R. Holden, *Classic Boats, No. 59*. 1993

D. Ings, *Penarth in Old Postcards, Volume 1* (1985) and *Volume II* 1990).

B. R. Keitch, *A Brief Look at Penarth*. Unpublished manuscript.

E. A. Lewis, *Welsh Ports Books*. 1927.

B. Lubbock, *The Log of the Cutty Sark*. 1949.

B. A. Malkin, *the Scenery, Antiquities and Biography of South Wales*. 1804.

M. Mabey, *The Windsors of Hewell Grange'*. 1984.

D. Moore (editor), *Barry: The Centenary Book*. 1984.
Wales in the Eighteenth Century. 1976

A. Morgan, *Porthcawl Legends*. 1974.

D. Morgan, *The Cardiff Story*. 1991

E. Mountford & N. Sprinks, *The Taff Vale Lines to Penarth*. 1993

J. Musselwhite, *The Butcher's Boys of Donkey Island*. 1980.

W. H. (Ben) Norman, *Tales of Watchet Harbour*. 1985.

F. J. North, *Glamorgan Historian, Volume 2*. 1965.

D. R. Paterson, *Early Cardiff Street and surrounding names*. 1921

Penarth Past & Present, *We Remember It Well*. 1994.

J. W. Perkins, *Building Stones of Cardiff*. 1984.

G. O. Pierce, *Placenames of the Dinas Powis Hundred*. 1968.

John & Stan Rendell, *Steepholm*. 1993.

Mr Rowlands, *Notes on old Penarth*. Unpublished monograph.

W. J. Slade, *Out of Appledore*. 1959.

G. Smith, *Smuggling in the Bristol Channel*. 1989.

Capt. W. H. Smythe, *Bute Docks: Nautical observations*. 1940.

P. Stuckey, *Sailing Pilots of the Bristol Channel*. 1977.

R. E. Takel, *The Story of Ports and Shipping*. 1982.

C. M. Tarver, *Penarth Yacht Club*. 1980.

Roy Thorne: *Penarth, A History, Volume One*. 1975
Penarth, A History, Volume Two. 1976

C. Tilney, *A History of the Parish of Penarth with lavernock*. 1964.

W. J. Trounce, *Cardiff in the Fifties*. 1918.

Captain White, *Admiralty Survey*, 1823-7.

W. P. Williams, *Windsor Monograph*. 1878.

Miscellaneous:
Cardiff Times
Log Books, Albert Road School
Penarth observer
Penarth Local Board Minutes (1875-1895)
Penarth Times
Penarth Urban District Council Minutes
Warings Penarth Map, 1868
Western Mail
Various Ordnance Survey Maps
Various Street Directories